AN INTRODUCTION TO THE WORLD'S

MAJOR RELIGIONS

A COLLEGE TEXTBOOK

AN INTRODUCTION TO THE WORLD'S

MAJOR RELIGIONS

A COLLEGE TEXTBOOK

David W. Atkinson

The Edwin Mellen Press
Lewiston/Queenston/Lampeter

Library of Congress Cataloging-in-Publication Data

Atkinson, David W.
  An introduction to the world's major religions

  Includes bibliographies and index
  1. Religions. I. Title.
BL80.2.A845   1988   291   87-28461
ISBN 0-88946-015-9

The Edwin Mellen Press
P.O. Box 450
Lewiston, NY 14092
U.S.A.

The Edwin Mellen Press
Box 67
Queenston, Ontario
CANADA L0S 1L0

The Edwin Mellen Press, Ltd.
Lampeter, Dyfed, Wales
United Kingdom SA48 7DY

Printed in the United States of America

TO MY MOTHER AND FATHER

CONTENTS

TO THE READER

If you are about to begin reading this book, the chances are good that you are a student in a first-year university world religions course. If you are, a few words of advice are perhaps in order.

This text contains a great deal of material, but this by no means suggests that you learn every detail. While the study of the world's religions demands. a thorough grounding in the teachings and beliefs of the various traditions, it also requires that you develop an understanding of the larger picture. It is this larger picture that is important to the individual believer, who, unless he is a professional theologian, likely cares little about the small details. What the individual believer does care about is what goes on within one to give a sense of religious completeness; this, it hardly needs saying, is something that goes beyond mere facts.

Because there seems so much material in this book, it is easy to fall into the trap of simply memorizing; if this is all you do, you will have learned very little. Question what you read; look at it in the context of your own experiences. Remember that religion is far more than facts and details; whatever religion you study, keep foremost in your mind that it is vital in the lives of many people.

Having said that this text contains much factual information, I may seem to contradict myself in asserting that it really only skims the surface. Indeed, any introductory textbook is necessarily selective, as the most complex issues are simplified and condensed down into a manageable form, and brutal decisions are made as to what to include and what to leave out. If you wish to get a true grounding in the study of the world religions, you must go much further than this book takes you. You must certainly learn more about the fabric of each tradition, and you must also read those who have thought deeply about what religion is. Always, however, what you read must be given thoughtful consideration as something more than mere academic pursuit. My hope is that this text will, if nothing else, stimulate you to look and think further; this, surely, is the ambition of anyone who writes an introductory textbook.

A number of individuals deserve recognition for the assistance they supplied in the writing of this book. Most obvious, of course, are my students, for whom this book was written in the first place, and who by their questions and responses suggested the general shape that this book has taken. Dr. Ronald Neufeldt of the University of Calgary, and Drs. Lawrence Lau and Tom Robinson of the University of Lethbridge offered useful suggestions for improving the manuscript. Ms Shelley Scott performed admirably as my Research Assistant in proof-reading the manuscript and in assisting in the preparation of the Index. Ms Linda Bryne also deserves thanks for assisting in preparation of the manuscript, and Mr. Glenn Tice should be recognized for the illustrations which appear at the beginning of each chapter. Mrs. Chris Lastuka deserves very special thanks for typing and formatting the manuscript; I greatly appreciated her skill and patience. Finally, I wish to thank Professor H. Richardson, General Editor of the Edwin Mellen Press, for his suggestions for improving the book.

AN INTRODUCTION TO THE WORLD'S

MAJOR RELIGIONS

A COLLEGE TEXTBOOK

CHAPTER I

INTRODUCTION

I

INTRODUCTION

WHAT IS RELIGION?

To study religion is to be faced with the issue of definition. What, one asks, is religion? The answer may seem simple enough, as we pull the dictionary from the shelf. Religion, Webster tells us, is "the feeling of reverence which is entertained towards a Supreme Being." It is "the recognition of God as an object of worship, love, and obedience."[1] Already, however, we are confronted with the problem that several of the great religions of the world do not recognize God as portrayed by its dictionary definition.

Buddhism, for example, is often talked about as a
non-theistic religion. Similarly, *Brahman*, which is the
absolute in much Hindu philosophy, is considered, not
as a personal deity, but as a final principle
underpinning the universe of change; and in Taoism,
the *Tao* is the "way" in which the universe unfolds. It
is obvious that Webster's definition is one that
recognizes the great religious traditions of the west --
namely Judaism, Christianity, and Islam -- but ignores
entirely the traditions of the east, such as Hinduism,
Buddhism, and Taoism.

It may be argued that the matter of definition
is best left until one has a familiarity with the world's
religious traditions: that one can define religion in a
general way only if one has knowledge of specific
religions. At the same time, if one is to approach the
study of religions intelligently, one must have some
preliminary understanding of what religion is. The
intention of this first chapter is to establish this basic
context.

Religion is, first and foremost, concerned with
the sacred, which the nineteenth-century Protestant
theologian Rudolf Otto defined as that which is
"wholly other" from ordinary existence.[2] To this end,
words used to refer to the sacred are often intended
to draw a contrast with what we know in any
ordinary or conventional sense. In Christianity, for
example, God is described as "infinite" and "eternal."
The point is that we cannot intellectually comprehend
"infinity," but we can understand finitude; the world
in which we live possesses finite dimensions. Thus to
talk of God as "infinite" is to refer to a reality that
is not characterized by finitude and is therefore
"wholly other" than anything we know. The same

argument can be made for the word "eternity," as our knowable world is one of time while God is outside time and, in fact, created it.

Virtually all religious traditions have words suggesting the "otherness" of the sacred. The spiritual goal of Buddhism is called *Nirvāṇa*, a Sanskrit word referring to the "blowing out" of the ignorance which fetters us to the suffering of *saṃsāra*. Given that all we know is ignorance and suffering, *Nirvāṇa* is a word that suggests "something" totally different from anything experienceable at the level of "ordinary" reality. Another Sanskrit word, *śūnyatā*, also refers to the Buddhist spiritual goal. The word means "emptiness," and indicates how the "totally other" of the sacred is being emptied of everything that defines us as limited human beings.

Concomitant with the notion of the divine as "otherness" is that of the divine as "ultimacy," which suggests everything other than the partiality we know and experience. As that which is ultimately real, the sacred is the source of all things which, by comparison, are conditional to it. Sometimes this source is presented as a divine creator who consciously and purposely forms the universe in which we live. This is the case, for example, in the three great monotheistic traditions of the west, Judaism, Christianity, and Islam. At other times, the sacred as source is an absolute principle by which the universe evolves. The Chinese religion of Taoism, for example, sees the *Tao* as that from which all things come.

Religion is, however, not only concerned with defining the sacred or talking about origins. More than anything else, religion maps out a way to experience the sacred. Regardless of whether one talks

of Christianity, Judaism or Hinduism, there is the
recognition that the individual is alienated from the
sacred and thereby experiences a pervasive sense of
incompleteness. This incompleteness is, in turn, the
cause of the frustration and anxiety inescapable in our
lives.

If one reflects on daily life, one gets a sense of
this incompleteness and anxiety. No matter what we
struggle to achieve, whether it be to earn an "A" on
an examination, to get a university degree, or to find
a good job, we are never satisfied: there is never a
moment when one can say, "I am contented." From
the perspective of religion, these mundane expressions
of incompleteness and dissatisfaction are symptomatic
of our alienation from the divine; put another way,
our daily tribulations result from being separated from
what is absolutely real. The Fall in the Genesis
account of Eden is a story of how humankind lost
God and the paradise enjoyed in living complete with
God. That Adam and Eve were expelled from Eden
with the injunction, "in the sweat of thy face thou
shalt eat bread,"[3] underpins the struggle and
frustration that is at once a feature of life and a
result of alienation from the divine. Similarly, the
existence of *avidyā* or ignorance explains in the Hindu
tradition how the individual *ātman* or "self" is
separated from the unity of *Brahman*, and thereby
trapped in *saṃsāra*, or the never-ending cycle of
mundane existence.

To say that religion directs one to experience
the sacred, therefore, is to say that religion outlines a
path by which the completeness of the sacred can be
realized. This path, which comprises the fabric of
religion, takes all manner of forms--mythology, ritual,

theology, ethics--but all are related in that they serve as a vehicle by which alienation from the sacred is overcome. Thus in Christianity, happiness and security are achieved in one's renewed relationship with God through Christ, while in Buddhism, *Nirvāṇa* is to be liberated from the ignorance and thirst that produces *duḥkha* or "suffering," and in Taoism to follow the *Tao* is to be freed from the self-imposed feelings and perceptions that are the source of our frustration. Simply put, religion provides ultimate meaning in a world characterized by shifting perceptions of reality.

RELIGIOUS STUDIES: BACKGROUND AND PURPOSE

This text approaches religion from the perspective of Religious Studies, which, as an academic discipline, is not very old. This is not to say, however, that scholars have only just come to the study of religion; during the Middle Ages and Renaissance, for example, theology comprised the very center of the university's curriculum. Rather, Religious Studies looks at religion in a way different from other more established disciplines such as theology and philosophy, even while taking from these disciplines. In this regard, Religious Studies is still evolving and looking to find its place in today's secular university, which is committed to exposing its students to the immense diversity of human endeavour and experience. Crucial issues for scholars are the scope, aims, and methodology of Religious Studies that make it distinctive and legitimate as an academic discipline. Before one looks at specific religions, therefore, one should look at some of the basic "ground rules" by

which Religious Studies operates, and be familiar, as
well, with how some of the other disciplines from
which Religious Studies has grown address the
spiritual dimension of humankind.

RELIGION AND THEOLOGY

The word "theology" originates with the Greek
word *theologia*, which is made up of two small words,
theos meaning "God" and *logos* meaning "discourse."
The most accurate meaning of the word "theology" is
that it is a "discourse" on God and God-related
matters. To this end, theology, as the systematic
consideration of what originates in religious experience,
is ruled by principles of consistency, proof, and
argument. Theology is not, however, intended as a
replacement for faith, nor is faith intended as a
jumping off-point for where theology breaks down.

Important is that theology is the exercise of a
committed believer, who works from within a tradition
to demonstrate by logical deduction the superiority of
one set of religious truth claims over another. A
Christian theologian aims, for example, to demonstrate
that Christianity is superior to other traditions.
Theological difference exists, moreover, as much within
traditions as among them. Calvin, in the sixteenth
century, tried to demonstrate that the claims of the
Roman Catholic Church were wrong while those of the
Reformed Churches were correct. There are, of
course, "theological breaking points" beyond which
theology cannot go simply because human reason has
its limitations. Here theology gives way to other
kinds of religious experience and expression.

Devotion, for example, is that dimension of religious life dwelling on the personal relationship of the individual with God; it is to love God and to believe that one is loved by God. Not surprisingly, theology, with all of its attendant complexities, is often subsumed to devotion and its emphasis on the simplicities of prayer and worship. Indeed it is not at all inaccurate to say that theology has very little direct effect on the devotional lives of individuals, albeit theology remains to supply the intellectual bedrock of any religious tradition. Suggestive is how two individuals, say Protestant and Catholic, can pray together, while at the theological level there are seemingly insurmountable differences between their traditions.

Mysticism is another form of religious experience running counter to theology. Plunging beyond all that characterizes one as a finite human being, the mystical experience is the direct, unimpeded recovery of oneness with the divine. Necessarily, then, the mystical experience opposes the intellectual fabric of theology because it can never be articulated. Mystics are found in virtually all the world's great religions: there are Christian mystics such as John of the Cross and St. Teresa of Avila, the Ṣūfis mystics of Islam, the Jewish mysticism of the *Kabbalah*, and the *yogins* of the Hindu tradition.

One final point ought to be made. Correctly speaking, the word "theology" should only be used in connection with theistic religions; after all, it is a discourse about God. But word meanings tend to change. Thus theology now refers to the intellectual systematization and justification of any religious tradition from inside that tradition. So, for example, one talks about Buddhist theology, even though, strictly speaking, Buddhism does not recognize a deity in the same way theistic religions do.

RELIGION AND THE SECULAR DISCIPLINES

What are referred to as the "secular" disciplines, notably anthropology, sociology, psychology and philosophy, treat religion in a way very different from theology. While theology gives one particular religious expression special status as authoritative, the secular disciplines reject outright that religion of any sort has special status because it deals with the sacred. Rather they see religion as a form of human experience to be treated like all other forms of human experience. Religion is considered, not as a way of understanding the sacred, but as a way of learning more about human beings and about how human beings function in society.

There are any number of "classical" examples that demonstrate this approach to religion. The famous sociologist Emile Durkheim (1858-1917), for instance, viewed religion as an expression of social obligation. For Durkheim, religion comprises an ideal passed on from generation to generation through a process of education, socialization, and enculturation. This ideal of behaviour does not originate with the divine, even though it is seen as sacred, but is the objectification of what exists in the consciousness of the individual. Religion is a mechanism of social control, and explains how and why society works as it does. While Durkheim was interested in religion and society, the psychoanalyst Sigmund Freud (1856-1939) saw religion as a way of explaining individual human behaviour. For Freud, religion originates in the human fear of what cannot be understood. The prototype for religion is found in the child-parent relationship and particularly the relationship between father and son. Just as the child finds protection and security in the parent, the adult finds similar protection and security in God as a parent figure.

The philosopher of religion, while not approaching religion as does the sociologist or psychologist, also differs radically in his approach from the theologian, although it is also the case that the philosopher gives the theologian many of his intellectual tools. The theologian accepts the truth of a religion; the philosopher, however, asks whether religion is true. In the western philosophical tradition, for example, much of the philosopher's time is taken up with arguing for or against the existence of God.

A good example of such a proof is the argument from first cause, which was recounted by the great medieval theologian and philosopher, Thomas Aquinas (1224-1274). According to Aquinas, everything that occurs has a cause, and this cause is in turn the result of a cause. Eventually, however, one reaches the point where there is no further cause. That which has no cause is God. Another of these arguments is the argument from design, which William Paley (1743-1805) articulates in his *Natural Theology: or Evidences of the Existence and Attributes of the Deity collected from the Appearances of Nature* (1802). The basis of Paley's argument is that the universe is like a watch, which requires a watchmaker who puts all the complex parts together into a functioning machine and then keeps it going. God, for Paley, is the watchmaker, who, not only creates the universe, but also maintains it.

For every argument proving the existence of God, there are, of course, others looking to prove the opposite. For example, David Hume (1711-1776), in his *Dialogues Concerning Natural Religion* (1779), counters the design argument by asserting that in infinite time, the universe will eventually come together in a way suggesting order. Arguments for and against the existence of God are not, moreover, the only concerns of philosophers of religion. Also prominent among the issues they consider are the validity of religious experience, the problem of evil, the nature and function of religious language, and the possibility of immortality.

RELIGION AND RELIGIOUS STUDIES

In looking at religion, Religious Studies takes from disciplines such as anthropology and sociology, and is, in this regard, both multidisciplinary and interdisciplinary. The dangers of drawing from these other disciplines are not inconsiderable. Most obvious is how these secular disciplines tend to reduce religion to something other than itself. Concentrating on the social and psychological functions of religion ignores the distinctive nature of the sacred which sets religion apart from other "human phenomena." This is not to deny that such approaches are useful; indeed they are essential if we wish to understand religion and religious life in the fullest possible context. But they can never replace how a religion must be allowed to speak on its own terms without particular disciplinary presuppositions.

A response to the secular disciplines is what is called the phenomenological approach to religion, which stresses careful description of the ways human religiosity is expressed. This approach is scrupulously objective, as each religion is described from the perspective of the impartial observer. But to assert this position is also to misrepresent religion, for what the particular believer accepts as true is vital in a way no other religion can be. One cannot ignore this vitality; for the believer, religion is the feelings and actions that go beyond mere description. What Religious Studies does, then, is retain the intellectual rigor of the secular disciplines, while appreciating the importance of religion to the believer. And to this "mix," it adds several ingredients of its own.

First, Religious Studies makes no distinction among religions with respect to truth. It is not a matter of one religion expressing the truth or expressing a greater degree of truth than another. Rather it is a matter of all religions being true for the orthodox believers of those traditions. Religious Studies adopts the perspective that Hinduism is true for a Hindu, Buddhism true for a Buddhist, Christianity true for a Christian, etc. Because one is an adherent in one tradition does not give one the right to judge other traditions false. No one denies, of course, that this is virtually impossible, as one never fully escapes one's own religious tradition or the tradition that shapes one's cultural environment. One should still, however, aspire to a kind of sympathetic objectivity, in which one puts one's biases and preconceptions on hold, for only by doing so will one get a reasonable appreciation of religious traditions different from one's own. This is not to say that Religious Studies aims to generate a crisis of faith in those committed to a particular tradition. If anything, one should come away from the study of other religions with the feeling that one's own religious life has been enriched, that by coming to understand and appreciate the religious lives of others, one has increased understanding and appreciation of one's own religious life.

This brings one to a second major feature of Religious Studies. When one studies a particular religion, one must aim to see the world as the orthodox believer sees it; one must, in other words, adopt the believer's world view or perspective. Only then will one gain an appreciation of what it means to be a believer or practitioner of a particular religion. While comparison is useful and often illuminating, one must avoid the tendency to see one religion as another. It is tempting, for example, to say that a certain Hindu idea or value is similar to a Christian idea or value, and from here to draw the conclusion that a Hindu is really a Christian. To keep things in the proper perspective, one should remember that the reverse could also be said. It is wise to remember that one religion is not another, and that in many respects differences are far more interesting than similarities.

Religious Studies as a discipline is an amalgam of approaches and attitudes. To understand a religion demands, not that one simply take it apart, but that one see and appreciate the integrated way in which religion looks outward at the world. One cannot study a religion without understanding its historical context, its theological foundation, its social and ethical teachings, its mythology, and its rituals. One of the values of Religious Studies in the university curriculum is that it values integration over particularities, the whole over the parts. This is not to say that the scholar of religion is a generalist without specific skills; on the contrary, he or she must possess a whole battery of skills. The scholar who studies religion must have the hermeneutical skills of the literary critic; must possess linguistic skills because, after all, the texts of the world's great religions are not originally written in English; must have the philosophical skills that allow for an intellectual understanding of religious experience; and must have the conceptual tools of the anthropologist and sociologist. Only then can the scholar understand what it means to talk about the "religious person." Beyond these things, the central issue in the study of religion is a critical sensitivity to what others believe and feel. It is in learning to appreciate the fullness of a particular religious approach to the world that one acquires the ability to integrate rather than to take apart. Analysis is still important, but it must never be seen as an end in itself.

A revealing analogy is between how one approaches religion and how one approaches a piece of literature. Although one might analyze a poem, taking it apart into its component parts, seeing how its images work and how it uses rhyme and rhythm, this analysis ultimately aims to heighten one's aesthetic experience of the poem as a single integrated whole. The aesthetic experience is one which goes beyond objective intellectualization in such a way that our individuality is merged with what we see or hear. Certainly we have all had the experience of being lost in a piece of music or immersed in a painting or sculpture. Approaching religion is not unlike approaching a piece of literature, and it is hardly surprising, therefore, that the aesthetic and the religious are often linked, as through art, humankind has, if not actually grasped the divine, at least been given a hint of divine nature. Thus the sublime leads to the sacred in Michaelangelo's Sistine Chapel and Jayadeva's *Gīta Govinda*, as well as in the Psalms of David and the Song of Solomon.

There can be no real objectivity in religion, for religion leads into a mystery where the conventional way of seeing and doing things ceases to have relevance. Given that religion aims to bring about a radical transformation within the individual, there is really no way one can step outside oneself to be objective about such an experience. One can argue, too, that such objectivity is a fiction, that however we look at something we are invariably trapped by who and what we are. So to speak scientifically about religion, as some insist they can, is to reveal nothing about religion, although it might reveal something about how we need to look at religion and at the world in general. Religion will remain deeply personal, even though by studying religion we hope to get an understanding of that personal dimension. That religion addresses humankind's deepest needs and insecurities further suggests that an understanding and appreciation of culture comes through an understanding and appreciation of religion. So, even if one does not personally feel committed to a particular religion, one can nonetheless learn much about one's own culture that is inevitably underpinned by religion, or about the cultural backgrounds of others that equally rely on religion for their shape and substance.

It is true, of course, that there are many more varieties of religious expression than are considered in this text. But the decision to be selective was made to avoid the descriptive superficiality that often plagues introductory textbooks which try to cover too much. While fault might be found in the detail of some discussion, it is arguable that the vitality of a religious tradition is found, not only in its fundamentals, but also in the many enrichments that produce its uniqueness. "Living" traditions are chosen for the sake of manageability, and so that appropriate attention is given to traditions comprising a vital ingredient in the modern world. No one doubts the importance of Norse, Greek, or Egyptian religion. Indeed, western civilization would be severely lacking without the *Illiad* and *Odyssey* or the great Norse sagas. The so-called "ancient" religions that have passed out of existence are, however, the subject of another quite different book.

This text gives an introduction to a number of the world's major living religions. "Major" is a word used rather loosely here. It refers in part to the number of adherents in a tradition. Thus Christianity with approximately 1,000,000,000 followers, Hinduism with about 500,000,000 and Islam with about the same number need no explanation. Taoism, however, has only about 31,000,000 adherents, and Judaism a mere 14,500,000. Here the word "major" is used in the sense that these religious traditions have had a direct and dominant influence on the development of a particular culture. Western civilization would not be what it is without Judaism, which has supplied much of its moral code; and the same can be said of the influence of Taoism on Chinese culture.

After all is said and done, one is perhaps still left asking why one should study religion. The answer is hardly obscure. Religion stands at the root of so much of the misunderstanding and conflict found in

the world today. As recently as thirty or forty years
ago, religion was largely limited by geography; only
infrequently did the practitioner of one religion come
into contact with the practitioner of another. But as
the world grows smaller, and as religious and cultural
pluralism becomes the norm rather than the exception,
this kind of religious isolation no longer exists. It is
quite conceivable that one's neighbours are from a
radically different religious tradition than one's own.
If communication is truly to take place with our
neighbours, then, it becomes necessary that we open
ourselves to how they see the world, even if
communication takes place only across the backyard
fence. Discrimination and bigotry are the product of
ignorance, and how often, one might ask oneself, has
one criticized another's religion because it makes
demands which one finds odd or unacceptable. It
may well be impossible to overcome the differences
between one religion and another, and to put aside
completely the notion that my religion is true and
your religion is not. But more and more scholars and
religious leaders are confronting the issue of
interreligious dialogue, looking to find in such dialogue
enrichment and not confrontation. This is an
ambitious goal, but it is well worth pursuing, even for
those coming to the study of the world's religions for
the first time.

Notes

[1] *The   Consolidated-Webster   Encyclopedic
Dictionary* (Chicago: Consolidated Publishers, 1954).

[2] Rudolf Otto, *The Idea of the Holy*, trans. John
W. Harvey (1958; rpt. London: Oxford University
Press, 1977), p. 36.

[3]Gen 3:19.

Selected Readings

Aquinas, Saint Thomas. *Treatise on God.* Trans. James F. Anderson. New Jersey: Prentice-Hall, 1963.

Aquinas, Saint Thomas. *St. Thomas Aquinas: Selected Writings.* Ed. M.C. D'Arcy. London: J.M. Dent and Sons, 1964.

Calvin, John. *A Reformation Debate.* Ed. John C. Olin. Michigan: Baker Book House, 1976.

Christ, Carol P. and Judith Plaskow. *Womanspirit Rising: A Feminist Reader in Religion.* San Francisco: Harper and Row, 1979.

Dasgupta, S.N. *Hindu Mysticism.* Delhi: Motilal Banarsidass, 1977.

Ellwood, Robert, S. *Introducing Religion from Inside and Outside.* New Jersey: Prentice-Hall Inc., 1978.

Freud, Sigmund. *Moses and Monotheism.* Trans. Katherine Jones. New York: Vintage Books, 1955.

Freud, Sigmund. *On Creativity and the Unconscious.* New York: Harper and Row, 1958.

Hume, David. *Dialogues Concerning Natural Religion.* New York: Hafner Publishing, 1969.

Hume, David. *The Natural History of Religion.* London: Adam and Charles Black, 1956.

Kaufmann, Walter. *Critique of Religion and Philosophy.* New York: Doubleday and Co., 1961.

Marx, Karl and F. Engels. *On Religion.* New York: Schocken Books, 1964.

Norbeck, Edward. *Religion in Human Life.* New York: Holy, Rinehart and Winston, 1974.

Otto, Rudolf. *Mysticism East and West.* Trans. Bertha L. Bracey and Richenda C. Payne. New York: The Macmillan Company, 1960.

Otto, Rudolf. *The Idea of the Holy.* Trans. John W. Harvey. Toronto: Oxford University Press, 1939.

Paley, William. *Natural Theology.* New York: The Bobbs-Merrill Co., 1963.

Saint John of the Cross. *The Living Flame of Love.* Trans. David Lewis. London: Thomas Baker, 1934.

Spencer, Sidney. *Mysticism in World Religion.* Gloucester, Mass.: Penguin Books, 1971.

Stone, Merlin. *When God was a Woman.* New York: Dial Press, 1976.

Tillich, Paul. *The Dynamics of Faith.* New York: Harper Torchbooks, 1957.

Toynbee, Arnold Joseph. *An Historian's Approach to Religion.* Oxford: Oxford University Press, 1979.

CHAPTER II

HINDUISM

II

HINDUISM

INTRODUCTION

Hinduism is the world's oldest living religion, with roots tracing back to at least 2000 BCE. Although there are Hindus living throughout the world, and in some concentration in the West Indies and South East Asia, Hinduism is for the most part limited to India where it began. As anyone who has visited India knows, Hinduism is comprised of an immense variety of religious expression, and to the outsider seems to have no internal coherence or thrust. This is at once true and not true. Hinduism has in

many respects operated like a vacuum cleaner,
scooping up all manner of influences and traditions
that cross its path. But Hinduism has also remained
true to a number of fundamental principles, despite
centuries of cultural and philosophical overlay. It is to
these principles that one must first go to understand
Hinduism.

BASIC CONCEPTS

Saṃsāra and Mokṣa

A distinctive feature of the Hindu tradition is
how it perceives time and history. There is no such
thing in Hinduism as a past once-and-for-all creation
leading to a future once-and-for-all end. Rather the
movement of things is cyclical: history is like the
turning of a wheel, which is conceived as always
having turned in the past and always turning in the
future. This perception of history as an ever-turning
wheel is in Sanskrit called saṃsāra ("duration"), while
one cycle of the wheel is termed a kalpa, or a "day of
Brahma," which lasts 4,200 million earthly years.
According to tradition, the great God Viṣṇu awakens
from sleep, and from the unfolding lotus petals coming
from his navel is born the god Brahmā, who then
creates the universe that Viṣṇu governs. The kalpa
ends with Viṣṇu falling asleep and the created
universe being absorbed once more into his body.

A kalpa is also talked about as a series of one
thousand lesser cycles called mahāyugas. Each of these
mahāyugas maps out the process of evolution and
devolution that characterizes the universe. At the top
of each mahāyuga is total moral and spiritual

awareness, at least as it is attainable in mundane existence. The bottom of the cycle is the very opposite, with the universe immersed in moral and spiritual ignorance and corruption. Between the top and the bottom occurs a gradual process of degeneration or spiritual devolution, which, once bottom is reached, leads into a gradual process of regeneration or spiritual evolution. A *mahāyuga* is divided into four yugas respectively called *Krita*, *Treta*, *Dvāpara* and *Kali*, each of which marks out a period of increased corruption. The generally held view is that, at the end of the *Kali Yuga*, the world will be destroyed before the cycle rights itself. The world is at present in the *Kali Yuga*, which has a duration of 432,000 years, and began in 3102 BCE with the conclusion of the war recounted in the Hindu epic the *Mahābhārata*.

While *saṃsāra* pertains to the unfolding of the cosmos, it also refers to the process of life-death-rebirth by which the individual is tied to multiple lives in the cycle of existence. In this context, the Hindu ambition or goal is to put an end to rebirth. This escape from *saṃsāra* is called *mokṣa*, or "liberation," which, as a spiritual experience that frees one from the fetters of worldly existence in life, anticipates how with death one achieves the ultimate liberation of no further rebirth.

Brahman and Ātman

To achieve *mokṣa* is, in the Hindu tradition, to experience *Brahman*. The word *"Brahman"* is derived from the Sanskrit root *"brh"* meaning "to grow" or "burst forth," and originally it meant "prayer," as in the bursting forth of speech. Later on, *Brahman* came to mean the ultimate cosmic principle from which the universe "bursts forth"; as the oneness that underpins the universe, it is the ground of being from which all particulars are derived.

In the *Upaniṣads*, which comprise the most important collection of Hindu philosophical texts, *Brahman* is also described with the word "*saccidānanda*," which is itself derived from three separate words: "*sat*" or "being," "*cit*" or "consciousness," and "*ānanda*" or "bliss." "*Sat*" refers to *Brahman* as absolute, unqualified being: it affirms that *Brahman* alone exists and is comparable or replaceable by nothing else. "*Cit*" suggests how *Brahman* is complete, omniscient awareness. *Ānanda* refers to the ecstasy that is *Brahman* and that is experienced in apprehending *Brahman*.

Finally, *Brahman* is talked about as both a cosmic ideal and an acosmic ideal. As a cosmic ideal, *Brahman* is said to be comprised of all particulars and that the "oneness" of *Brahman* is the underpinning harmony that transforms them from disparate particulars into a single all-pervasive whole. Such an understanding of *Brahman* is intended when the writer of the *Śvetāśvatara Upaniṣad* observes that *Brahman* "is all this, what has been and what will be . . . the lord of immortality."[1] To achieve *mokṣa* is to experience the "all this"; more particularly, it is to experience one's *ātman* or innermost eternal self as part of divine harmony. This is what is meant by the *Upaniṣadic* teaching, "*ātman* is *Brahman*." One way of looking at this understanding of *Brahman* is to see creation as a symphony of many notes playing in harmony with one another. The self is just one of these notes, but, because we insist on seeing it as the most important note, we have no sense of the entire symphony.

When *Brahman* is considered as an acosmic ideal, it is talked about as the transcendental dimension that defies all characterization and description. The "oneness" of *Brahman* goes beyond particulars, denying their independent reality. While having an existence in the phenomenal world, particulars are the result of superimposing names and forms on the unitary, formless reality of *Brahman*. To say "*ātman* is *Brahman*" in this case is to talk of the extinction of the fiction of individual selfhood in the unity of *Brahman*. Thus in the *Kaṭha Upaniṣad* is written, "He who has perceived that which is without sound, without touch, without form, without decay, without taste, eternal, without smell, without beginning, without end, beyond the Great, and unchangeable, is freed from the jaws of death."[2]

That there should be two such opposing views of *Brahman* in the *Upaniṣads* should not be construed as problematic, for the *Upaniṣads* are speculative in nature and not dogmatic assertions of truth, although it is also true that later philosophers in the Hindu school of *Vedānta* devoted much time to finding a reconciliation between the two views. Both suggest that the reason one is fettered to *saṃsāra* is that one gives too much importance to self and fails to realize that all is ultimately one regardless of how this oneness is talked about. It is because we are ego-centered in everything we do that we suffer the anxiety of existence. One does everything for oneself, and is therefore subject to the ever-present feeling that one may lose what one possesses or fail in what one does. Failure in this sense affirms the unimportance of self, and produces a psychic conflict between what is the case and what we wish were the case. What is demanded, then, is that we see things from the perspective of the oneness that is *Brahman*, and thereby free ourselves from the limited ambitions and values that we think are so important, but which, because they have no ultimate value, are the root cause of our problems.

Māyā and *Avidyā*

To define *mokṣa* as a radical transformation of perception whereby one directly apprehends the oneness of reality demands an explanation of how individual ego centeredness comes about in the first place. The failure to apprehend the oneness of *Brahman*, and the tendency to see instead a world of particulars in which self is the most important particular, is described by the word "*māyā*" or "fiction." *Māyā* is to see things, not as things actually are, but as we think they are through the veil of our ego centeredness. This *māyā* is produced by *avidyā* or "ignorance," which may be further defined as *vyāvahārika-satya* or "lower knowledge." As the way in which we function at an everyday level, *vyāvahārika-satya* is the intellectual understanding requiring that things be taken apart; as such, it works against the unity that is the ultimate reality of *Brahman*.

One is quite justified in asking if there is any real difference between the terms "*māyā*" and "*avidyā*"; indeed many commentators treat them as synonymous. What is important is that both terms affirm how apprehension of *Brahman* is a non-discursive immediate plunging to absolute reality: this is *pāramārtha-satya* or "higher knowledge." What they also suggest is how in Hinduism the intellect is often seen as hiding rather than revealing truth, although here one must avoid making blanket statements. As we shall later see, the achievement of *mokṣa* demands that we use what is available to us in the world. It is therefore not a matter of not using the intellect, but of using it in such a way that it helps us achieve our goal.

Dharma and *Karma*

Two additional concepts in the Hindu tradition are *dharma* and *karma*, which together comprise the pistons that drive the ever turning cycles of *saṃsāra*. *Dharma*, which comes from the Sanskrit *"ḍhr"* meaning "to sustain," refers to who and what one is: it is the sum total of one's weaknesses, strengths, potential, etc. *Karma* originally referred to the rituals prescribed in the earliest Hindu scriptures, the *Vedas*. It has, however, come to take on the second meaning of any action that brings forth a reaction. Here an action is not limited to something overt such as a physical action; it also includes those emotional and psychological activities that are internal to the individual.

Put together, *dharma* and *karma* offer an explanation for rebirth in *saṃsāra*. It is *karma* or action which determines *dharma* or who one is. A simple way to remember this is that a person who overeats becomes overweight; it is not a matter of a person beginning overweight and then overeating. So it is that the actions of one lifetime will determine one's rebirth in another lifetime: one reaps the benefits of a moral life and pays the price for an immoral one. Moral and immoral are very simply explained. Moral actions are unselfish actions; immoral actions are selfish ones. If one lives a life of selfishness, one will be reborn at a level of life more appropriate for such behaviour; the same holds true for one who lives an unselfish life. The action of *karma* and *dharma* must not, however, be construed as a kind of mechanistic determinism. No matter how bad one gets, it is always possible to turn things around; one never becomes so engrossed in one's self that freedom of choice is absolutely taken away. And there is always the optimistic note that all sentient creatures will eventually achieve *mokṣa*, as one remains in a lower life form for only as long as it takes to burn off the bad *karma* accrued in previous lifetimes.

HINDUISM IN HISTORICAL PERSPECTIVE

The history of the Hindu tradition conveniently falls into a number of periods characterized by particular religious developments. This does not mean, though, that there is ever a single point at which one period becomes another. History is a matter of one thing giving rise to another, and certainly this is the case in the Hindu tradition, as each religious development is inevitably an outgrowth of or a response to what went before.

The Vedic Period (2000 BCE - 600 BCE)

The Vedic Period begins with the infiltration of the Āryans into India about 2000 BCE, although some scholars suggest an earlier date. While little is known about these Āryans, they likely originated in eastern Europe around the area of the Black Sea. The Āryans were not the first civilization in India but replaced a much older civilization, commonly known as Indus because it was situated along the Indus River System, or Harappān after Harappā, the site of significant archaeological finds. The Indus civilization was comprised of highly developed city dwellers, while the conquering Āryans were nomadic. The earliest expression of the Hindu tradition is likely a fusion of the religious beliefs of the Āryans, who also brought into India the classical language of Sanskrit, and those of the indigenous Indus.

The Vedic Period produced three great collections of scripture, which to the orthodox Hindu are known as *śruti* ("that which is heard"). These texts contain eternal truths, and are to be distinguished from *smṛiti* ("that which is remembered"), which is made up of texts that can be placed in historical time and place. The earliest of the *śruti* are the *Vedas*, which focus on the ancient practices of sacrifice. The word *Veda* comes from a Sanskrit original meaning "knowledge"; therefore, the *Vedas* convey knowledge pertaining to the sacrifice.

The *Vedas* themselves are further subdivided into four collections or *Saṃhitās*. The oldest of these is the *Rig Veda*, dating from about 1500 BCE. It derives its name from the Sanskrit word *"ric"* meaning "hymn"; thus the *Rig Veda* is a collection of hymns in praise of the gods. Typical of such hymns is the following Hymn to Rudra, which celebrates the god's powers of destruction and healing:

Of what is born, you, Rudra, are the most glorious in glory, the strongest of the strong, with the thunderbolt in your hand. Carry us safely to the farther shore of anguish; ward off all attacks or injury.

We would not wish to anger you, Rudra
the bull, by acts of homage or ill praise, or
by invoking you together with another god.
Raise   up   our   heroes   with   your   healing
medicines; I hear that of all healers you are
the best healer.

If someone should call with invocations and
oblations, thinking, "I will appease Rudra
with songs of praise"--may the soft-hearted
god who is easy to invoke, the tawny god
whose lips are full--may he not suspect us of
that and give us over into the power of his
anger.[3]

The next oldest of the *Saṃhitās* is the *Sāma
Veda*, probably compiled several hundred years after
the *Rig Veda*. The *Sāma Veda* contains *samans* or
chants used in connection with the sacrifice to the
gods. Of about the same age as the *Sāma Veda* is the
Yajur Veda, which contains *yajus* or brief explanations
of the sacrifice said by the priest as he works his way
through the rituals.

The *Atharva Veda* is significantly different from
the other three collections. The *Rig Veda, Sāma
Veda*, and *Yajur Veda* focus on the sacrifice as
performed by the *hotars*, a highly specialized group of
priests. These rites came to be known as *śrauta* rites.
The *Atharva Veda*, dating about 1000 BCE, is much
less sophisticated. Contained within it is the poetry of
the *Atharvans*, who might be seen as unschooled
practioners catering to the religious needs of the
people in their homes rather than in the sacred
confines of the temple. The prayers of the *Atharva
Veda* deal with all manner of things: prayers to cure

illness, prayers for a son, prayers to protect against demons, etc.

The second great collection of texts produced during the Vedic Period is the *Brāhmaṇas*, written about 800 BCE. These texts are commentaries on the sacrificial ritual central to the *Vedas*, and have as their purpose the controlling or at least the influencing of *Brahman*. The *Brāhmaṇas* were the work of the priests, and display a complexity that was often criticized by the other classes for removing ritual sacrifice from the warp and woof of Hindu religious practice. As well, the priests, by virtue of their special function in the sacrifice, were elevated to god-like status and further criticized for losing touch with the religious life of the ordinary people.

There are also discernible trends in the *Brāhmaṇas*, as well as in the *Vedas*, which anticipate the next great group of texts, the *Upaniṣads*, which were for the most part written between 800 and 600 BCE, although some appear as late as the fifteenth century CE. While in the *Vedas* there is a recognition of many gods, there is also implicit reference to the underpinning unity of all things. This is further expressed in the symbolism of the sacrifice, as well as in the way the many gods are in time subsumed to the one god, Agni or "god of the sacrificial fire." One of the most important expressions of this unity is the story of the primal person or universal *Puruṣa* recounted in the *Rig Veda*. Through the self-sacrifice of the *Puruṣa*, who represents the unmanifested potential of creation, the phenomenal universe of particulars comes into being.

Thus the ancient writers were faced with what has become a philosophical chestnut, the problem of

the one and the many. This problem, as we have
already seen, looms large in the *Upaniṣads*. As well
as the most important philosophical texts in the
Hindu tradition, the *Upaniṣads* also stand as a
reaction to the increasing complexity of Brahmanic
religion, and may be seen as a reinterpretation of the
Vedas rather than as a further commentary on the
Brāhmaṇas. The *Upaniṣads* stress personal experience
over the rigor of Vedic ritual, and, in that they were
often written by the governing class or *Kṣatriyas*, they
suggest a revolt against Brahmanic authority.

As the final development of Vedic religion, the
112 *Upaniṣads* are referred to as *Vedānta* or "end of
Veda," and in this regard one *Upaniṣad* is attached to
one of the *Saṃhitās*. The *Upaniṣads* collectively,
however, by no means present a consistent,
homogeneous philosophy, as significant divergences
exist between one *Upaniṣad* and another, and even
within a single *Upaniṣad*. It is not so much that the
Upaniṣads supply definitive answers; rather they probe
to find a coherent view of the universe not found in
either the *Vedas* or the *Brāhmaṇas*. In a way
appropriate to speculative works, the *Upaniṣads* are
written in dialogue form as a student asks the
question which the *guru* or "teacher" answers. Here
some scholars see the Sanskrit word "*Upaniṣads*" as
having particular significance. Made up of three words,
"*ṣad*" -- "to sit", "*upa*" -- "under", and "*ni*" --
"beneath," "*Upaniṣads*" describes the situation of the
student sitting at the feet of the master.

What must be stressed is that the three groups
of texts, the *Vedas*, the *Brāhmaṇas*, and the
Upaniṣads, really address the same issues, even while

having significantly different orientations. The *Vedas* are works of mythology in the sense that mythology is the imaginative expression of religious truth. In grappling with questions of ultimate reality, the writers of the *Vedas* use language that hinges on metaphor and suggestion rather than logic and intellectual consistency. The *Brāhmaṇas*, as works focusing on the sacrifice, stress the importance of religious ritual, which is the re-enactment in the practioner's immediate religious life of the archetypal event recounted in myth. Through ritual the practitioner participates in the significance of the original myth. Finally, the *Upaniṣads* are at once a rational and mystical consideration of divine unity, and it is out of this reflection that came such concepts as *Brahman* and *ātman*. Especially important about the *Upaniṣads* is that they are very much a philosophical hinge for the entire Hindu tradition, for, not only do they grow out of earlier Vedic and Brahmanic religion, but they also serve as the philosophical basis for virtually all subsequent development within the Hindu tradition.

One final thing needs mentioning here. While the *Brāhmaṇas* and *Upaniṣads* are very different groups of texts, another small group of texts, the *Araṇyakas*, serve as a link between the two. Basic to the *Brāhmaṇas* is the view that the physical performance of the sacrifice is concomitant with internalized mental activity. In time, it came to be accepted that the paraphernalia of the sacrifice existed quite separately from the mental ritual performed by the priest, and that the mental ritual did not, in fact, require the actual performance of the sacrifice. Thus the individual became much more important, as did the techniques of meditation and reflection basic to the *Upaniṣads*. The texts which stressed the mental performance of ritual were called the *Araṇyakas* or "Forest Books" because their contents were taught and practised in forest retreats. These *Aranyakas*, then, serve as a transition between the mythological-ritualistic orientation of the *Vedas* and *Brahmanas* and the philosophical speculation of the *Upaniṣads*.

The Epic Period (600 BCE - 200 CE)

The Epic Period is so named because it produced the two great epics of the Hindu tradition, the *Mahābhārata* and the *Rāmāyaṇa*. Much of the material found in the *Mahābhārata*, which is much the longer of the two works, dates from as early as the sixth or seventh century BCE, although it did not reach its final form until about 200 CE, while the material of the *Rāmāyaṇa* may be as old as 1000 BCE, although it too did not reach a final form until around the turn of the common era. The story lines of the two works are quite different. The *Mahābhārata* focuses on a conflict over succession between two sides of the same family, the Kurus and the Pāṇḍavas, while the *Rāmāyaṇa* recounts the great king Rāma defeating Ravana, the king of Ceylon. Both works are similar, however, in being the combined efforts of many poets over a long period, and, although each has a central unifying story, both contain a whole array of tales revealing much about Indian life and culture.

The Growth of Theism

The Epic Period is characterized by a number of specific developments. Most obvious is the growth of religious theism, in particular Śaivism or the worship of Śiva and Vaiṣṇavism or the worship of Viṣṇu. Both Śaivism and Vaiṣṇavism stress the love of God as a major ingredient of religious life, and thereby further signal the declining status of the sacrifice. While Śiva and Viṣṇu dominate as the major deities, the theism of the Epic Period is also characterized by a dizzying array of other deities, which are seen as personal incarnations or "*avatāras*" of the supreme god, who remains the undifferentiated *Brahman* of the *Upaniṣads*. Important to understanding this perception of the divine is the *Bhāgavata Purāṇa*, which is one of a host of later (c.400-1200 CE) texts comprising the Purānic literature that, like the *Mahābhārata* and *Rāmāyaṇa*, is significant for containing material about the gods not contained in the *Vedas*.

According to the *Bhāgavata Purāṇa*, Absolute Reality possesses three phases:[4] *Brahman, Bhāgavat,* and *Paramātman. Brahman* is defined as the impersonal, undifferentiated absolute which cannot love or be loved. The *Bhāgavat* is the absolute as Lord, who possesses personal characteristics, and loves and is loved. Finally, *Paramātman* is a partial manifestation of *Bhāgavat*; it is a particular form of *Bhāgavat* as manifested in the many gods of the Hindu pantheon. Viṣṇu and Śiva are each envisioned as *Bhāgavat*, the Lord who is at once personal and impersonal, a god of features yet also beyond differentiation. In turn, Śiva and Viṣṇu as *Paramatman* appear as *avatāras* to perform particular functions as circumstances demand.

Although shrines to Śiva appear as early as the first century BCE, the recognition of Śiva as the one supreme God does not really take hold until the

eighth century CE. As revealed in the popular image
of Naṭarāja or the dancing Śiva, he is seen as at once
the creator, preserver, and destroyer of life. The
creative aspect is particularly venerated, and to this
end the central object of worship in temples to Śiva is
a stone pillar representing the male generative organ
(*lingam*) implanted in the female organ (*yoni*). As
well, there are those who worship the *śakh* or the
"Great Goddess," who is seen as the world creating
and world controlling aspect of Śiva. This *śakh* is
most often called Durgā, although it is also known by
such names as Kālī, Umā, and Pāravatī.

The god Viṣṇu appears in the Vedas as a
fertility god, but, like Śiva, does not become
prominent as the one God until well into the common
era. Viṣṇu is most often worshipped as one of his ten
avatāras. Of these *avatāras*, Kṛṣṇa and Rama are by
far the most important, and, in fact, Kriṣṇa in some
forms of Vaiṣṇavism becomes himself the supreme
God.

The Importance of Duty

A second major development of the Epic Period
to signal the decreasing importance of the sacrifice is
a new emphasis on practical religious instruction
stressing duty and moral living. Religion is no longer
the sole purview of the priests, but is part of ordinary
daily life. Significant here is how Hinduism, while still
seeing *mokṣa* as the ultimate goal, recognizes that one
must live in the world and indeed enjoy life without
being consumed by it.

To this end, a major teaching is the "Four
Ends of Man," which define the basic categories of

human endeavour. These ends are *dharma*, which determines one's obligations in society; *artha*, which outlines how one goes about the business of material gains; *kāma*, which refers to the pursuit of physical pleasure; and *mokṣa*, which is the pursuit of liberation. Not everyone pursues these ends in the same way, as Hinduism keeps foremost the uniqueness of each individual. At the same time, however, the need for specific instruction results in a formal rationalization of human behaviour in what is known as the *varṇa-āśrama-dharma*. This rationalization is the primary focus of a group of texts called the *Dharma Śāstras*, written between the 6th and 2nd centuries BCE, of which the most influential is the *Manava-Dharma-Śāstra*, attributed to the great lawgiver Manu.

According to Manu, Hindu society is divided into four classes or "*varṇa*": *Brahman* or priest, *Kṣatriya* or soldier, *Vaiśya* or middleclass, and *Śūdra* or lower working class. Depending on which class one is born into, itself dependent on the *karma* of previous lifetimes, the individual has particular responsibilities in society. Thus Manu writes:

> But for the sake of the prosperity of the worlds, he [God] created the Brahman, the Kṣatriya, the Vaiśya, and the Śūdra to proceed from his mouth, his arms, his thighs, and his feet. . . .

> To Brahmans he assigned teaching and studying (the Veda), sacrificing for their own benefit and for others, giving and accepting (of alms).

The Kṣatriya he commanded to protect the people, to bestow gifts, to offer sacrifices, to study (the Veda), and to abstain from attaching himself to sensual pleasures.

The Vaiśya to tend cattle, to bestow gifts, to offer sacrifices, to study (the Veda), to trade, to lend money, and to cultivate land.

One occupation only the lord prescribed to the Śūdra, to serve meekly even these (other) three castes.[5]

While Manu saw all four classes as necessary to the effective running of society, there is no question that *varna* contained within it the seeds of social discrimination, particularly with respect to the *Śūdras*. The distinction was made, for example, between the *Śūdras* and the three upper classes, who were classified as *dvijas* or "twice born." *Śūdras* were excluded from practicing Vedic ritual, while the three upper classes were "born again" in being given access to the sacred texts. Thus in time *varna* became a mechanism for social repression justified on the grounds of *dharma*. If one is of an impoverished lower class, it is *dharma* as determined by previous action or *karma*. Such is also the case if one lives a life of comfort and affluence; that too is the result of *karma*. It was such thinking that led to a devolution of the class system into something called *jāti* or "caste", which is often identified as the worst product of a corrupted Hindu tradition. Significantly, the great Hindu reformers of the nineteenth and twentieth centuries worked to eliminate caste, and discrimination on the basis of caste is today prohibited by law in India.

Āśrama, the other major component of *varṇa-āśrama-dharma* teachings refers to stage of life. The young boy formally enters the first stage of life, *brahmacārin* or "studentship," at the age of 8 if a *Brahman* and 12 if a *Kṣatriya* or *Vaiśya*. He goes through the *Upanāyana* ceremony in which he receives the sacred thread and is formally given to a *guru* or teacher, with whom he will study the Vedic texts for a number of years. Instructions for the student are many and explicit; the following is typical:

He who has been initiated shall dwell as a religious student in the house of his teacher . . .

Twelve years (should be) the shortest time (for his residence with his teacher).

A student who studies the sacred science shall not dwell with anybody else than his teacher.

Now (follow) the rules for the studentship.

He shall obey his teacher, except when ordered to commit crimes which cause loss of caste.

He shall do what is serviceable to his teacher, he shall not contradict him.

He shall always occupy a couch or seat lower than that of his teacher.

He shall not eat food offered at a sacrifice to the gods or the Manes.

Nor pungent condiments, salt, honey, or meat.

He shall not sleep in the day-time.

He shall not use perfumes.

He shall preserve chastity.

He shall not embellish himself by using ointments and the like.

He shall not wash his body with hot water for pleasure.

But, if it is soiled by unclean things, he shall clean it with earth or water, in a place where he is not seen by a Guru.

Let him not sport in the water whilst bathing; let him swim motionless like a stick.

. . .

Let him not look at dancing.

Let him not go to assemblies for gambling, &c., nor to crowds assembled at festivals.

Let him not be addicted to gossiping.

Let him be discreet.

Let him not do anything for his own pleasure in places which his teacher frequents.

Let him talk with women so much only as his purpose requires.

Let him be forgiving.

Let him restrain his organs from seeking illicit objects.

Let him be untired in fulfilling his duties;
Modest;
Possessed of self-command;
Energetic;
Free from anger;
And free from envy.[6]

At the end of his studentship, the boy, now a man, is expected to marry, establish his own household, take his place in society, and perform the Vedic rites of sacrifice. The *grihastha* or "householder", we are told,

. . . should ponder over what is good for the Self. He should not, as far as possible, neglect his duties in respect of the three ends of man, namely, virtue, material gain, and pleasure, at their proper times.

Learning, religious performances, age, family relations, and wealth--on account of these and in the order mentioned are men honored in society. By means of these, if possessed in profusion, even a shūdra deserves respect in old age.[7]

For most, the role of the householder will take up the remainder of life. When household responsibilities are largely satisfied, however, it is possible for the individual to embark on a third stage, that of the *vānaprastha* or "forest dweller." The forest dweller retires from active household life to practice austerities and meditation as a means of personal spiritual development:

When a householder sees his skin wrinkled, and his hair white, and the sons of his sons, then he may resort to the forest.

Abandoning all food raised by cultivation, and all his belongings, he may depart into the forest, either committing his wife to his sons, or accompanied by her.

Taking with him the sacred fire and the implements required for domestic sacrifices, he may go forth from the villages into the forest and reside there, duly controlling his senses.

Let him offer those five great sacrifices according to the rule, with various kinds of pure food fit for ascetics, or with herbs, roots, and fruit.

Let him wear a skin or a tattered garment; let him bathe in the evening or in the morning; and let him always wear his hair in braids, the hair on his body, his beard, and his nails being unclipped.

Let him perform the food offering with such food as he eats, and give alms according to his ability; let him honour those who come to his hermitage with alms consisting of water, roots, and fruit.

Let him be always industrious in privately reciting the Veda; let him be patient of hardships, friendly towards all, of collected mind, ever liberal and never receiver, and compassionate toward all beings. . . .

He should live without a fire, without a house, a silent sage subsisting on roots and fruit. . . .[8]

In contemporary times, the stage of forest dweller is a time for spiritual reflection, in which one determines whether one is adequately prepared to embark on the fourth stage of *āśrama*, that of *sannyāsin* or "world renouncer," or whether it is more appropriate that one return to the life of householder. Instead of retiring to the forest as in the past, one might now go to a temple or *āśram* to reflect on the future direction of one's life. If one feels truly committed to the spiritual life, one embarks on the stage of *sannyās* that is entered by means of formal ritual in which one renounces all worldly ties, including wife and family. This ritual is really a funeral in which an effigy of the would-be *sannyāsin* is burned on a funeral pyre to signify the death of the worldly person. In becoming *sannyāsin*, the individual also relinquishes his sacred thread, given him when he went through the ceremony of the twice born, and thereby signifies that he is totally removing himself from ordinary society. The *sannyāsin* takes a new name, wears only a loin cloth and an ochre robe, and has as his only possessions a staff, a water jar, and a begging bowl. Enjoined to the three restraints of silence, action, and mind, the *sannyāsin* single mindedly pursues release from *saṃsāra*. The *sannyāsin*, Manu says, delights

. . . in what refers to the Soul, sitting in the postures prescribed by Yoga, dependent on external help, entirely abstaining from sensual enjoyments, with himself for his only companion. . . .[9]

Obvious in the *varna-āśrama-dharma* is that it largely centers on the male. This is not to say, however, that women were ignored. Marriage was considered the *Upanāyana* ceremony for a girl, for, in being given to a husband, she was also being given to her *guru*. If men completed the normal twelve-year period of Vedic study, they were typically twenty to twenty-five when they married, while girls, at least during the period of the *Dharma Śāstras*, had very often not reached puberty. Thus the notion that the husband would be teacher to his wife is not all that inappropriate. This dependency on the husband gradually grew until it was generally accepted that women acquired merit from their husbands. A daughter's marriage, was, therefore, a serious business, and great care was taken that the "right" husband was found. Especially important was that the class of husband and wife were compatible.

Paths to Liberation

In addition to the *Dharma Śāstras*, one other text looms large in addressing the matter of religious instruction. The *Bhagavad Gītā* or *Song of God* recounts, in a dialogue between the god Kṛṣṇa and the prince Arjuna, the several *mārgas* or "paths" to enlightenment. Underpinning these *mārgas* is a particular understanding of the psychological makeup of the individual, or what is called the *guna* or empirical self. According to traditional teaching, the *guna* self is comprised of three components, *sattva*, *rajas*, and *tamas*. *Sattva* refers to purity, lightness, and knowledge; *rajas* to passion; and *tamas* to inertia. Those individuals who possess a *sattvic* personality, in other words, those in whom *sattva* is the dominant feature, are given to intellectual pursuit, while those with a *rajic* personality are given to action, and those with a *tamic* personality tend to be "laid back" and relaxed. Too much of any one component is a bad thing. For example, too much *rajas* produces a person who spends most of the time running around, very often with little forethought or planning, while too much *tamas* produces someone who is lazy. At the same time, however, Hindu philosophers point out that *rajas* is necessary for the universe to run, just as *tamas* is necessary to hold the universe together.

In that these three components comprise the individual, it is these components that must be used to expedite liberation. Here the Hindu philosophers point to three tendencies in the individual corresponding to the three *gunas*. There is the human tendency to knowledge corresponding to *sattva*, the human tendency to action corresponding to *rajas*, and the human tendency to contemplation corresponding to *tamas*. The problem is that these human tendencies are misdirected: one pursues the wrong knowledge, one carries out the wrong actions, and one is given to laziness rather than to constructive reflection. What is necessary is that one direct these tendencies in such a way that they lead towards *mokṣa* and not away from it, and to this end Hinduism supplies particular paths that one can follow depending on one's personality type. These paths, as outlined in the *Bhagavad Gītā*, are not exclusive, although certainly one path might dominate in an individual possessing a particular psychological makeup.

Karma Mārga

Karma Mārga or the "path of action" requires that one pursue *Karma Yoga*. The word *yoga* is from the Sanskrit "*yukh*" meaning "to yoke" or "to get control of." Thus *Karma Yoga* is a discipline which leads to control of action; it is the way of work. The ideal of *Karma Yoga* is disinterested action in which one has no concern for the fruits of one's actions: to realize this ideal is to achieve *mokṣa*. In daily life, one works towards this ideal by pursuing unselfish action, in which one puts the other before the self. *Karma Yoga* is, then, a way of overcoming through action the egocentricity that is in opposition to the oneness of *Brahman*. Important in *Karma Yoga* is the *varṇa-āśrama-dharma* in that it largely translates into tangible human action what the pursuit of disinterested action entails.

Bhakti Mārga

The path of *Bhakti* or "love of God" demands the pursuit of *Bhakti Yoga*. Underpinning this *yoga* is the view that from the contemplation of the perfection and glory of God there comes an exploding of the egocentricity that chains the individual to *samsāra*. Fundamental to *Bhakti Yoga* is the belief that the individual without God is worthless and that whatever worth an individual possesses comes from what God extends to him or her. So it is that *Bhakti Yoga* is expressed through love of God and faith in the capacity of God to help one who is unable to help oneself. It is also the discipline pursued by one in whose personality *tamas* is the dominant *guna*. In traditional Hindu teaching, such a personality tends to be emotional rather than one given to intellectual reflection or activity in the world. Love for God, then, becomes a way of using the emotions as a means of achieving liberation from the ego-centeredness expressed through self love.

The most tangible expression of this love of God is *pūjā* or worship, which entails prayer and offerings to God. *Pūjā* itself has a number of forms. There is the *pūjā* carried out by the householder alone, usually in the early morning, there are the devotions carried out by husband and wife together, and there is the more elaborate *pūjā* performed at the temple or in association with the festival of a particular deity.

Jñāna Mārga

Appropriate for the *sattvic* personality is *Jñāna Mārga* or the "path of knowledge." *Jñāna Yoga* demands that the individual search for a true knowledge of things which is the knowledge of the undifferentiated ultimate reality of *Brahman*. To achieve this knowledge, which is the higher knowledge of *pāramārtha-satya*, one must see the impermanence and ineffectualness of the things of the world, and thereby overcome the lower knowledge of *vyāvahārika-satya*. To know *Brahman*, however, requires more than the simple discrimination of knowledge, and here meditation, sometimes called *Raja Yoga* or the "royal way," plays a crucial role.

The most important exponent of meditation in the Hindu tradition is Patañjali, who produced the *Yoga Sūtras* sometime during the first centuries of the common era. According to Patañjali, *yoga* is *citta-vritti-nirodha*, or the "the suppression of mind," which leaves one freed of individual identity and aware only of the absolute consciousness of *Brahman*. This *yoga* has eight distinct stages, which can be grouped under three general headings: moral preparation, control of body, and control of mind.

It is understood that one cannot just plunge into the practice of *Raja Yoga*; one must first prepare for the demands this path imposes. Therefore there is a period of preparation entailing two stages. First one pursues *Yama* or "restraint," by which one abstains from violence, theft, falsehood, and greed; and second one adheres to *Niyama* or "observance," which entails the pursuit of purity, study, and honour of God. To a certain degree, *Yama* and *Niyama* correspond to *Karma Yoga* and *Bhakti Yoga*, which to some "purists" are seen as mere preparatory steps in the discipline of *Raja Yoga.*

In that so much of the mind is controlled by the body, *Raja Yoga* teaches that the body be brought under control and that the mind be liberated from it. This requires a further three steps. *Āsana* or "sitting" demands that the meditator adopt particular postures. While some *yogins* go to extreme lengths, most adopt the simple position of sitting with legs crossed and hands folded on top of the lap. The purpose of *Āsana* is, not to strain the body, but to find a posture in which it is possible to forget the body. Next one must practice *Prāṇāyāma* or "breath control." Breathing is the one thing we perhaps least control. By restricting inhalation, retention, and exhalation, the *yogin* has another way to get control of the body. Once having this control of the body, the *yogin* can withdraw from it in *Pratyāhāra* by breaking contact with the world and being left only with the mind to worry about.

Needless to say, the mind is a notoriously difficult thing to control; personal experience tells us that the mind goes all over the place, doing whatever it wants to do. So it is that the *yogin* now looks to direct the mind in a final series of three steps. In *Dhāraṇa* or "concentration," the *yogin* concentrates on an object; it can be anything, although very often it is the image of a favorite deity. But it is one thing to concentrate on something and another to keep one's concentration there. Therefore through *Dhyāna* one stabilizes one's mind on the object so it does not move away from it. Finally, one achieves the stage of *Samādhi* or "wisdom," which is to experience *Brahman.* This final stage has, however, several steps of its own. First, there is the suppression of subject.

Initially the mind is conscious of itself apprehending the object; thus in this stage the subject is removed, leaving only consciousness of object. Finally, there is suppression of object. *Brahman* is undifferentiated oneness while the object, of which there is consciousness, is a distinction. At this stage, the object is suppressed leaving the unimpeded consciousness which is *Brahman.*

Sūtra Period (600 - 1400 CE)

This is the period of great philosophical flowering in the Hindu tradition. Although devotionalism continued as a dominant force in Hinduism during this period, men of more reflective bent backed up from their tradition to place it into a philosophical context. The result of this intellectual reflection is the Six Orthodox Schools. While the ideas of the schools and even the schools themselves had been around for some time, it was during the so-called Sūtra Period that they were formally systematized. Briefly the schools are as follows.

Nyāya

Nyāya refers to "right reasoning," and is therefore the science of demonstration. It is a form of logic, and supplied a way of looking at knowledge which to greater and lesser degrees was accepted by the other schools. The school originates with Gautama's *Nyāya Sūtras* in the third century BCE with important commentaries written by Vātsayāyana and Uddyotakara in the fourth and sixth centuries CE respectively.

Vaiśeṣika

Vaiśeṣika is a philosophy of "particulars" which classifies all objects of experience into six categories: substance, quality, activity, generality, particularity, inherence, and non-existence. Originally non-theistic, *Vaiśeṣika* later introduced God as presiding over and controlling the particulars of the universe. The school begins with the *Vaiśeṣika Sūtras* of Kanāda.

Sāṃkhya

Sāṃkhya is notable for its evolutionary theory. It reduces all categories into two. *Prakṛti*, as the source of all objective reality, exists with the three constituents of *sattva, tamas*, and *rajas* in a state of dynamic equilibrium. The *Puruṣa* is the omnisicient soul which, by coming into contact with *Prakṛti*, disturbs its dynamic equilibrium and thereby begins the evolutionary process that results in the empirical self. *Māyā* is the result of the *Puruṣa* mistaking itself for the empirical self of *Prakṛti*, while *mokṣa* is to return to the undifferentiated state of the omniscient *Puruṣa*. The earliest work on *Sāṃkhya* is the *Sāṃkhya-kārikā* of Iśvarakṛṣṇa written in the fifth century CE.

Yoga

Although *yoga*, as we have seen, refers to a great many practices, it especially refers to the school founded by Patañjali in the second century BCE. *Yoga* and *Sāṃkhya* are often linked in that *Yoga* supplies a method or technique by which the evolutionary process of *Prakṛti* can be reversed so that the unimpeded *Puruṣa* can be realized.

Pūrva Mīmamṣā

Pūrva Mīmāmsā is a school of interpretation which examines the relation between the expressed word and the idea the word expresses. It is, in other words, a form of hermeneutic. The first codifier of Pūrva Mīmāmṣā is Jaimini in the fourth century BCE, with important commentaries by Prabhākara (650 CE), and Kumārila Bhatta (700 CE).

Uttara Mīmāmṣā or Vedānta

Vedānta comprises the most important system of Hindu philosophy, and today it remains a living force in the tradition. The source for Vedānta is, of course, the Upaniṣads, although the earliest commentary is Bādarāyana's Vedānta Sūtras, written sometime between 500 BCE and 200 BCE. Others, in turn, wrote commentaries on the Vēdanta Sūtras. Among these are Śankara in the eighth century, Rāmānuja in the twelfth century, and Madhva in the fourteenth century, all of whom differ radically in their interpretation of the Brahman-ātman relationship. Śankara in Advaita Vedānta ("Non-dualism") claims that ātman is a fiction and that only Brahman is ultimately real, while Madhva in Dvaita Vedānta ("Dualism") claims the opposite, insisting that Brahman and ātman are independently real. Rāmānuja in Viśiṣṭādvaita Vedānta (qualified non-dualism) takes the middle road, claiming that the self is real but is only one particular in the totality of Brahman.

Neo-Scholastic Period (1400-1800)

After the great philosophical flowering of the Sūtra Period, the Hindu tradition went into a period of gradual decline. A major cause of this decline was the intellectual bankruptcy of the tradition, as philosophers came to be more interested in argument and debate for its own sake rather than for what it contributed to larger religious issues. Although the philosophical stream of a religion may not immediately touch the lives of a religion's ordinary practitioners, it nonetheless supplies a foundation for a tradition which gives it stability and substance. Without that philosophical stream, Hinduism gradually degenerated into a religion of excess and superstition, and the great glories of the ancient Hindu heritage were forgotten, even by priests and *gurus*.

The situation was not helped, moreover, by the presence in India of Muslim invaders, who first appeared in the eleventh century and for a period of nearly six centuries dominated the Indian subcontinent. While Islam had little direct effect on Hinduism, the fact is that it indirectly inhibited religious and cultural growth by offering a religious alternative to the Indian people. Indeed, many Indians, especially in the north, converted to Islam and this eventually resulted in the separate nation of Pakistan. At the greatest expanse of the Moghul empire under Aurangzeb (1618-1707), only the far south of India remained under Hindu rule.

After the death of Aurangzeb, the Moghul Empire declined rapidly and India was left in chaos. The nations of Europe were quick to take advantage of the situation, although in the give and take of European expansionism Great Britain quickly came out on top. With the defeat of the French at the Battle of Plassey in 1757, Britain gained control of the province of Bengal through the East India Company, which gradually extended its sovereignty over an ever-widening extent of Indian territory. In time the mercantile interests of the East India Company came into conflict with the political interests of the British government, and eventually in 1858 the control of India was taken over by the British "Government of India." The English introduced into India English law, English education, and English technology, and the result was a new threat to traditional values and beliefs, especially as even the Indians themselves saw that if they wanted to get on in life they must become Anglicized.

Hindu Renaissance (1800 - present)

The final chapter of the history of Hinduism is still going on, entailing as it does a desire by Hindus to find again the greatness of their own tradition. By 1800 Hinduism had degenerated into a hodge podge of beliefs, a caste system that perpetuated social repression, a Brahmanic class that lived off the ignorance of the common people, and bizarre excesses such as widow burning in which the dead man's wife was expected to jump willingly on her husband's funeral pyre and thereby accrue the very best kind of *karma*. As well, the Indian population was beset by a cultural, intellectual, and political malaise, feeling that it would never escape from beneath foreign domination.

In the early eighteenth century, however, one finds the beginning of an attempt to refind Hinduism's past glory. This movement, called the Hindu Renaissance or the "rebirth" of Hinduism, was a natural result of other events in India. The British colonial government found that India was simply too large a country to administer without Indian help.

Thus there developed a highly educated Indian class, who served in the British Colonial bureaucracy, very often in positions of considerable importance. While members of this educated class were certainly immersed in British and European culture, it was only a matter of time before they turned to their own Indian tradition to discover that it was in any number of ways older and richer than its European counterpart.

Crucial in this Renaissance was Rāmmohun Roy (1772-1833), who, as the first of the great religious and social reformers, is often described as the "Father" of the Hindu Renaissance. Rāmmohun Roy's major concern was that religion had degenerated into habit, as people blindly followed the dictates of the priests without any sense of religious vitality in their lives. Rāmmohun is also important because he typifies the many Hindu reformers that followed him. Taken up with the immediate need for change, he was not an especially systematic thinker, drawing as he did on all manner of sources as particular need dictated. He was familiar with Persian and Arabic literature, especially Aristotle and the *Qu'rān*, had spent time at Benāres studying the *Dharma Śāstras* with Hindu pundits, had gone through a period of "wandering," going as far as Tibet and the *lamas* of the great Buddhist monasteries, and, through his association with the English, become thoroughly grounded in the teachings of the New Testament. While rejecting the doctrinal framework of Christianity, Rāmmohun Roy was nonetheless profoundly effected by its ethical teachings. For a time, Rāmmohun was attracted to Unitarianism, but eventually left this group because of its close association with Christianity. Rāmmohun appreciated, however, the value of congregational worship, and out of this came the *Brāhmo Samāj* or "Society of Brāhmos," which stands as the first of a number of important reform groups of the Hindu Renaissance.

Another of the early reformers was Dayānanda Saraswatī (1824-1883). A born rebel, Dayānanda ran away from home several times as a child, and eventually on one such occasion did not return. Dissatisfied with his life, Dayānanda wandered for fifteen years throughout India as a *sannyāsin*. His travels revealed to him that the Hindu tradition was desperately in need of revitalization. Like Rāmmohun, Dayānanda pointed his finger at the *Brahmins* for using their position to keep the people in ignorance and superstition. Dayānanda was equally critical of Christianity, and in particular the missionaries who failed to realize the richness of the Hindu tradition, and who used their superior "colonial" status to impose their beliefs on Indians. Finally, like many others, he condemned the inertia of Hinduism, and despaired at how Hindus everywhere seemed hopelessly crushed.

Dayānanda went back to the *Laws of Manu* to demonstrate that class was not simply something of birth; it also entailed responsibility, which he saw the *Brahmins* as not fulfilling. He was also critical of the entire scholastic baggage of Brahmanic literature, which he saw imposing the Brahmanic system on people for whom it had no religious meaning. To counter such religious ignorance, Dayānanda interpreted the *Vedas* for himself, and disseminated the results of his work to all who would listen, including those classes that were traditionally excluded from Vedic study.

Like Rāmmohun Roy, Dayānanda surrounded himself with a group of likeminded persons. This group, called the *Ārya Samāj* or "Society of Noble Men," stood for the brotherhood of men, the equality of the sexes, the need for equal justice and equal opportunity, and love and charity towards all. It was also notable for its work in reconverting to Hinduism those who had left for Christianity or Islam. Taking a page from a book of the Christian missionaries, the *Ārya Samāj* became actively involved in philanthropic work, establishing orphanages, widows' homes, and schools, and contributing to famine relief.

While Dayānanda and Rāmmohun were largely social and religious activists, this is not to say that the rich philosophical heritage of India went ignored. Important in this regard is Vivekānanda (1863-1902), who stands as the first major missionary of *Vedānta* to the west. Like others, Vivekānanda felt that many of the social evils of his time were due to a stultified orthodoxy that the ordinary person neither understood nor appreciated. For there to be any spiritual awakening, Hindus must come again to the basic teachings, which, for Vivekānanda, were those of *Vedānta*, the philosophy of the *Upaniṣads*. To this end, Vivekānanda tried to express the teachings of *Vedānta* in a way meaningful to as many as possible; his intentions are very clear in the title of his little pamphlet, *Practical Vedānta*. Vivekānanda saw *Vedānta* as underpinning all forms of religious expression. Specific religions, he argued, are not exclusive of one another; rather one form of religious expression supplements another. He asserted that Divine Truth is so comprehensive that it is impossible for any one religion to concentrate on more than a few different aspects of it. While there may be contradictory views as one goes from religion to religion, this contradiction does not make one thing true and the other false: it is a matter of looking at the world from different points of view.

Another major figure who was both philosopher and social and political activist was Aurobindo Ghose (1872-1950), although Aurobindo's early life hardly seemed to prepare him for what was to come later. Aurobindo's western-educated father was adamant that his sons should be similarly educated, and to this end, he sent Aurobindo first to a convent school run by nuns, then to a private tutor in England, and finally to St. Paul's School in London. Aurobindo completed his education at King's College, Cambridge, where for the first time he encountered other Indians and learned something about his homeland. Aurobindo returned to India in 1892 to enter into the service of the Baroda State Government. He also immersed himself in Bengali, Sanskrit, Marathi, and Gujarati literature, and came to have an appreciation of the richness of his own tradition and of the need to free Indian culture from the fetters of colonialism. From the turn of the century, Aurobindo was drawn increasingly into politics; nationalism, for Aurobindo, became the call of God. Aurobindo was repeatedly arrested for his political activities, and, while imprisoned, experienced a number of extraordinary visions, which convinced him to leave politics for seclusion and yogic practice. Aurobindo remained silent for nearly thirty years after retiring to his aśram at Pondicherry. While his physical voice was silent, however, his pen was not, and this period produced an immense literary output.

Underpinning everything Aurobindo wrote was his notion of integral yoga, which, while consistent with earlier Hindu thinking, strikes out into new territory. Aurobindo stands opposed to any division between the spirit and the material universe, which he sees as a fatal flaw of philosophy. What is necessary is a perception of reality which does not demand that one choose between the spiritual and the material. This is to understand that humankind's upward desire for the divine is related to the descending movement of the divine in a process Aurobindo calls involution; in other words, it is because the spirit descends into life that life seeks something higher than itself. Everything, then, is a single unity, and what is required of the individual is to ascend by means of *yoga* through the various involutions of the divine until the undifferentiated unity of *Brahman* is once more realized.

Along with Aurobindo, two other figures dominate twentieth-century Hinduism. On the one hand is Rabīndranāth Tagore (1861-1941), the romantic idealist, who turned his back on political life to establish his school of Santiniketan at Bolpur north of Calcutta, and who to this day inspires Indians with his songs. poems, and paintings. On the other is Mohandas Gandhi (1869-1948), called *Mahātma* or "Great One" by Tagore, who was the foremost figure of Indian political life in the first four decades of the twentieth century, and who has left in his ideal of *satyagraha* a legacy of non-violent non-cooperation that has profoundly influenced the peace movement of contemporary times.

Tagore was born into a family long familiar with reform. His father Debendranāth was himself a significant religious reformer and a key figure in the Brāhmo Samāj, as to a lesser extent was his grandfather Dwarkarnāth. A man of incredible talents as dramatist, novelist, poet, philosopher, artist, and religious reformer, Tagore won the Nobel Prize for Literature in 1913 for his prose poems *Gitanjali* ("Song Offerings"), and in 1919 was knighted, although he subsequently returned his knighthood after the massacre at Amritsar. There is no one way to talk about Tagore's religious views, except to say that his so-called "Religion of Man" or "poet's religion" is a remarkable expression of religious humanism. Tagore saw creation as a divine arena of eternal evolution in which humankind experiences an infinite series of creative moments. For Tagore, *mokṣa* is not escaping from *saṃsāra*, as conventional teaching suggests; rather it is to experience the divine which is the world in its creative fullness. For Tagore, any kind of limitation is an evil, for he saw nothing as impossible to humankind; as we aspire for ever greater completeness, we experience the joy which each new moment brings. Not surprisingly, Tagore is remembered as a great internationalist who travelled throughout the world calling for new understanding. At Visva-Bharati, Tagore created a university where east could meet west, and where one could discover the world unhindered by dogma, orthodoxy, or any form of preconceived truth.

In contrast to Tagore, Gandhi was very much a pragmatist who lived in the world. After spending twenty-one years in South Africa championing the cause of Indian settlers there against economic and social discrimination, Gandhi returned to India in 1915 to become a leading figure in the Indian National Congress, the major organization working for Indian

home rule. Gandhi's great contribution as a political
leader was the way he merged political protest with
religious ideals. In this regard, one thing is paramount
about Gandhi: he was a man who worked in the
world with an attitude of selflessness and dispassion,
and represented in the purest sense what is intended
in the *Bhagavad Gītā* as the *Karma Yogin.*

Gandhi's ambition was freedom for India so
India could contribute to the world. But he insisted
that this freedom not be won with violence. Gandhi
believed the divine was best represented by the word
"truth," and he saw as a synonym of truth the
concept of *ahiṃsā* or "non-violence." Thus realization
of the divine in the world is to be achieved through
ahiṃsā in action, which demanded an effort to free
oneself from such feelings as anger, malice, hatred, and
jealousy, and to cultivate compassion, forgiveness,
generosity, and kindness. The political realization of
these moral ideals Gandhi called *satyagraha,* which
literally means "holding onto the truth." While
satyagraha includes such things as political agitation,
economic boycott, civil disobedience, and strike,
satyagraha must never be pursued with the intent of
hurting those whom one opposes, even if one is oneself
persecuted. Indeed, for Gandhi, the ultimate aim of
satyagraha is always concern for the other, as one
looks to make one's adversary see through error for
his own good.

As a religious thinker, it is difficult to
categorize Gandhi. One thing, however, is very clear.
In saying that "Truth is God," Gandhi indicates that
religion is not something expressed in only one way.
Gandhi accepted the universal law of *karma* that
determines who and what a person is. Therefore he

understood that all persons, being different, would find the divine in different ways. Gandhi believed that every religion contains good and bad. Thus all religion should be allowed and no one religion has the right to insist it possesses the truth alone. Indeed it was such thinking that lay behind Gandhi's profound tolerance for all manner of humankind.

CONCLUSION

At the beginning of this chapter, the remark was made that Hinduism is a disparate tradition, which, over its four-thousand year history, has drawn into itself all manner of religious expression. Even the sketchiest of historical overviews affirms this observation. This also, however, begs the question of what it means to be a Hindu. It is often said that Hinduism possesses an openness absent in many other religions: that Hinduism considers acceptable whatever brings an individual religious fulfilment. Its concepts of *dharma* and *karma*, which determine human difference, allow for varying religious responses, as does the view that religious expression, as a thing of this world, is conditioned by *māyā* and therefore is in no way absolute. Admirable as such openness is, it leads to the situation where it is really impossible to determine where Hinduism begins and ends.

What, then, can one identify as being specifically Hindu? First, there is its understanding of history, even though this might be said to be Indian rather than Hindu. Humankind is trapped in a realm of suffering, and therefore the end goal for all Hindus is to escape from this realm. Second, all Hindus accept the sacredness of the *Vedas* as depositories of divine truth. Whatever is important for humankind to know is found in these texts, and everything since the *Vedas* is a restatement of this divine truth in a way that humankind can understand. Third, the laws of *karma* and *dharma* are universally accepted by Hindus, even though in *bhakti*, for example, the importance of individual effort in achieving *mokṣa* is conditioned by a notion of mercy in which God helps one achieve what one cannot do alone. There remains in Hinduism the view that one must take responsibility for one's own actions, and that one can only blame oneself for whatever difficulties one incurs, either in this lifetime or in a future one. Finally, the acceptance of diversity might itself be identified as a major feature of Hindusim, for perhaps no other religion allows for such differences and indeed justifies them in its philosophical tradition.

Beyond anything else, however, Hinduism, like all religions, looks to bring completeness and peace to an individual alienated and alone in the world. It is not, of course, as if Hinduism never failed in its task; like any other religion, it has experienced its moments of great accomplishment and its periods of decline that are perhaps best forgotten. But there has always been a remarkable vitality to Hinduism that, even today in India, can be experienced in virtually any temple anywhere, as it looks to bring the individual into touch with the ground of being that provides completeness in the face of the changing vicissitudes of life.

Notes

[1] *Śvetāśvatara Upaniṣad*, in *Sacred Books of the East*, ed. F. Max Muller (1984; rpt Delhi: Motilal Banarsidass, 1975), XV, 247.

[2] *Kaṭha Upaniṣad*, in Ibid, p. 14.

[3] *The Rig Veda*, trans. Wendy Doniger O'Flaherty (Hammondsworth: Penguin, 1951), p. 221.

[4] Lee Siegel, *Sacred and Profane Dimensions of Love in Indian Traditions* (Delhi: Oxford Univresity Press, 1978), pp. 102-103.

[5] *Manu Smirti*; I and X, in *The Hindu Tradition*, ed. Ainslie T. Embree (1966; rpt. New York: Random House, 1972), pp. 79-80.

[6] *Apastamba Dharma Sūtra*, I, in Ibid, p. 85.

[7] *Yajñavalkya Smirti*, I, in Ibid, p. 88.

[8] *Manu Smirti*, IX, in Ibid, p. 91.

[9] Ibid., VI, p. 93.

Selected Readings

Agrawal, M.M. *The Philosophy of Non-Attachment.* Delhi: Motilal Barnarsidass, 1982.

Aurobindo, Sri. *The Secret of the Veda.* Pondicherry: Sri Aurobindo Aśram, 1982.

Babb, Lawrence A. *The Divine Hierarchy: Popular Hinduism in Central India.* New York: Columbia University Press, 1975.

Borthwick, Meredith. *Keshub Chunder Sen.* Columbia: South Asia Books, 1982.

Bowes, Pratima. *The Hindu Religious Tradition.* London: Routledge and Kegan Paul, 1977.

Carmody, Denise Lardner. *Women and World Religions.* Nashville: Abingdon Press, 1979.

Chennakesavan, Sarasvati. *Concepts of Indian Philosophy.* Madras: Orient Longman Ltd., 1976.

de Bary, William Theodore (ed.). *Sources of Indian Tradition.* 2 vols. New York: Columbia University Press, 1968.

Gandhi, M.K. *Non-Violence in Peace and War.* Ahmedabad: Navajivan Press, 1942.

Hiriyanna, M. *Outlines of Indian Philosophy,* 1932; rpt. London: George Allen and Unwin, 1968.

Jordens, J.T.F. *Dayānanda Sarasvatī: His Life and Ideas.* Delhi: Oxford University Press, 1978.

Kinsley, David R. *Hinduism: A Cultural Perspective.* New Jersey: Prentice-Hall, Inc., 1982.

Koller, John M. *Oriental Philosophies.* New York: Charles Scribner's Sons, 1970.

Moore, Charles A. (ed.). *The Indian Mind.* Honolulu: University of Hawaii Press, 1967.

Nag, Jamuna. *Rājā Rāmmohun Roy.* New Delhi: Sterling Publishers Ltd., 1972.

Naravane, Vishwanath S. *An Introduction to Rabindranath Tagore.* Missouri: South Asia Books, 1978.

Naravane, Vishwanath. *Modern Indian Thought.* New Delhi: Orient Longman, Ltd., 1978.

Nehru, Jawaharlal. *The Discovery of India.* Ed. Robert J. Crane. New York: Doubleday and Co., Inc., 1960.

O'Malley, L.S.S. *Popular Hinduism.* New York: Cambridge University Press, 1970.

Pandey, Dhanpati. *The Ārya Samāj and Indian Nationalism.* New Delhi: S. Chand and Co. (Pvt.) Ltd., 1972.

Puligandla, R. *Fundamentals of Indian Philosophy.* New York: Abingdon Press, 1975.

Raju, P.T. *The Philosophical Traditions of India.* London: Unwin Brothers Ltd., 1971.

Ray, Ajit Kumar. *The Religious Ideas of Rāmmohun Roy.* New Delhi: Kanak Publications, 1976.

Richards, Glyn. *The Philosophy of Gandhi.* New Jersey: Barnes and Noble Books, 1982.

Wilkins, W.J. *Modern Hinduism.* Delhi: B.R. Publishing Corp., 1975.

CHAPTER III

BUDDHISM

III

BUDDHISM

INTRODUCTION

Although Buddhism is no longer a major religion in India, it is in India that Buddhism has its roots. It begins with the enlightenment experience of the man Siddhārtha Gautama, who was born about 560 BCE in the region of Nepal in northern India. Gautama came from the tribe of Śākyas, and is therefore often referred to as Śākyamuni or "Sage of the Śākyas." Gautama's father, Śuddhodana, was ruler of the small kingdom of Kapilavastu, and, as a *Kṣatriya*, wanted his son to follow in his footsteps.

The legend suggests that, on the occasion of Gautama's birth, Śuddhodana consulted a number of learned sages, who prophesied that the child was destined for great things; hence he was given the name Siddhārtha or "he who has achieved his goal." The sages indicated that Siddhārtha's future could go in one of two directions. If he remained with the world, he would become a great ruler; if, however, Siddhārtha turned from the world, he would become a great religious teacher. Not surprisingly, it was Śuddhodana's intention that his son should follow him as king. Despite the king's every effort, however, he ended up failing to have his son become the great ruler he wished him to be.

To guarantee that Siddhārtha would not be tempted to take the spiritual path, Śuddhodana gave to the prince every conceivable worldly pleasure and did everything in his power to shield him from contact with the suffering and ugliness of the world. One day, however, Siddhārtha went for a ride with his charioteer, and saw a decrepit old man. Returning to the palace, Siddhārtha reflected on what he saw, and, in order to discover more, decided to take a second ride. This time, he saw a diseased man; and on a third trip, he saw a corpse. So it was that Siddhārtha experienced the impermanence and suffering of life for the first time. What he had seen bothered him a great deal. It is said that Siddhārtha, in reflecting on suffering, achieved the first meditative state (dhyāna), and that, as a result of this experience, he decided to look for answers to the questions of what causes suffering and how this suffering can be alleviated. Thus Siddhārtha, in an event referred to as the Great Renunciation, left his wife and young son in the middle of the night, and rode out of the palace with his charioteer. Siddhārtha sent the charioteer back to the palace, and then, after cutting off his hair, exchanged clothes with a passing hunter.

Siddhārtha first studied with some of the great teachers of India, and although he mastered everything they taught him, he still felt dissatisfied. Next Siddhārtha joined with a group of ascetics, and for a number of years followed a path of rigorous abstinence and asceticism. Here too Siddhārtha failed to find answers to his questions. Thus he turned to a third way, which entailed meditation along the lines of *Raja Yoga*. Settling himself beneath a great fig tree, which comes to be called the *bodhi* tree (*bodhi* meaning "wisdom"), Siddhārtha vowed not to move until he had achieved enlightenment. In due course, after repulsing various temptations, Siddhārtha's mind broke through the confining fetters of conventional existence to achieve Supreme Enlightenment, as Siddhārtha himself was transformed from an ordinary man into the Buddha or "one who has awakened."

Tradition has it that Siddhārtha initially had reservations about returning to society, but eventually concluded that he must tell others how they too could achieve supreme spiritual liberation. This path, which the Buddha preached for the next forty-five years, comprises the essence of Buddhism. In particular, the Buddha challenged what he saw as the deadness of Brahmanic religion, and in this regard Buddhism may be seen as a reaction to the ritual complexity of Brahmanic religion just as were the *Upaniṣads*. The difference is that, while the writers of the *Upaniṣads* continued to recognize the *Vedas* as eternal truth, Buddhism is an outright rejection of all Hindu scriptures.

SPREAD AND DEVELOPMENT
OF BUDDHISM

Soon after the Buddha's death, or what is
properly called the "Great Nirvāṇa," Mahākāśyapa
called the Buddha's followers together for what has
come to be known as the First Great Council. Little
is really known about the historical circumstances of
the Council, and, like much else about early
Buddhism, we have been left with an idealized account
that is at once history and legend. Held at Rājagṛha
about 485 BCE, the Council aimed to determine the
content of the Buddha's teachings. The result was the
first two of the three collections or Piṭakas ("Baskets")
of the Buddhist canon, although scholars have
determined that some of the individual works
purportedly coming from the council are later
additions. The two piṭakas are the Dharma or
"teachings of the Buddha" and the Vinaya or "rules
of monastic discipline." Two of the Buddha's disciples
are said to have figured prominently in the
proceedings. First, Upāli recited the rules of the
Vinaya; and second, Ānanda recited each of the five
Nikāyas or "collections" of sūtras comprising the
Dharma. A particular feature of the Vinaya and
Dharma is that they were not recited in Sanskrit but
in an early form of Māgadhī, which is the language of
Aśoka, India's first Buddhist emperor, thus further
signifying Buddhism's break with the dominant Hindu
tradition.

While there was general agreement at the First
Council as to what the Buddha said, it did not take
long before there was serious disagreement over what

the Buddha meant. Although tradition suggests there was a breakup into eighteen different schools of Buddhism, it is generally agreed that there were more than thirty such schools, each tending to emphasize or interpret particular aspects of the Buddha's teachings in a way slightly different than the other schools. Why these differences came about is a matter of scholarly conjecture, although a number of obvious reasons come to mind. Śākyamuni did not leave behind a successor who could exercise authority over what constituted valid teaching, and, given the Buddhist emphasis on meditation and individual initiative, it is hardly surprising that different people interpreted the Buddha's teachings differently. As well, India in the fifth century BCE was a place of tremendous intellectual ferment, and, even though Śākyamuni specifically warned against metaphysical speculation, Buddhism did not remain immune from what was going on around it. The Buddha's teachings were talked about and debated like any other teaching of the time, and inevitable differences of opinion resulted. Finally, the Buddhist scriptures were not written down until about the first century BCE. That the scriptures were passed down orally meant that certain texts were known by some and not by others, and that different perceptions of the Buddha's teachings grew out of stressing one set of texts over another. These differences among early Buddhists are expressed in the third of the *piṭakas*, the *Abidharma* or "Higher *Dharma*." The term "*Abidharma*" refers at once to the specific commentaries of one school, and more generally to the entire corpus of commentaries produced by all the schools between about 350 BCE and the 5th century CE.

To combat the schism that was coming to characterize early Buddhism, a Second Council was called at Vaiśālī in 383 BCE. Rather than overcoming differences, however, the Second Council led to the polarization of the various schools into two groups, the *Sthaviras* or those who followed the "teachings of the elders" and the *Mahāsanghikas*, who were more liberal thinking in their interpretation of the Buddha's teaching than the *Sthaviras*. The *Sthaviras* encountered yet more metaphysical disagreement and, as a result of a Third Council at Pāṭaliputra in 250 BCE, divided into the *Vibhajyavādins* and the *Sarvāstivādins*. While the *Sarvāstivādins* died out about 1000 CE, the *Vibhajyavādins* continued in Ceylon as *Theravāda*, which remains today as one of the two great Buddhist groups. The *Mahāsanghikas* gradually evolved over several hundred years into *Mahāyāna*, which comprises the second great Buddhist group. *Theravāda* is the Buddhism found in Sri Lanka (Ceylon) and S.E. Asia, while *Mahāyāna* is the Buddhism of China, Tibet, Korea, and Japan and Vietnam.

THE FOUR NOBLE TRUTHS[1]

After his enlightenment, the Buddha is said to have preached to the ascetics with whom for a time he had practised austerities. The Buddha's sermon, traditionally called the Deer Park Sermon, is important because it contains the Four Noble Truths, which, regardless of whether one is *Theravādin* or *Mahāyānist*, comprise the most fundamental of Buddhist teachings.

The first of the Noble Truths is the Noble Truth of *duḥkha*, which is usually translated as "suffering," but which might better be thought of as the anxiety and discontentment of human existence. According to the Buddha, all that comprises human existence is touched by *duḥkha*. This is not to say that humankind cannot enjoy life, but that what we identify as pleasure still leaves us dissatisfied. When the Buddha talks of *duḥkha*, he gives a number of examples. Some of these are obvious: suffering is sickness, suffering is death, suffering is association with the unpleasant and dissociation from the pleasant. Perhaps not so obvious is the Buddha's remark that birth is suffering, for here he points to the insatiability of human desire, which is initiated by birth and which is acted out in everything we do. It is part of being human that we are never satisfied; we always want something more, and this unsatisfied desire is *duḥkha*.

In the Second Noble Truth the Buddha addresses the origin of *duḥkha*, which he identifies as thirst or craving. Our lives are consumed with thirst: when we are sick, we wish to be healthy; when we are poor, we want to be rich; even when we are rich, we want to be richer. All this "specific" kind of craving points, however, to a fundamental craving, the craving for self. We are ego-centered creatures; hence, every action we take, every thought we have, affirms for us our individual identity. This, the Buddha claims, is a mistake.

Crucial to understanding why the Buddha makes this claim is the concept of *anitya* or "impermanence." It is the nature of the universe that everything is flowing away and hence everything is impermanent. It is a very natural thing to accept this notion of impermanence when looking outwards at the external world. What we find difficult is accepting the notion of impermanence when we turn our gaze inwards. Therefore we hang on to the notion that, despite all evidence to the contrary, there is some core of our being that remains the unchanging witness of everything else. To affirm this sense of individual being, we do everything we can to inflate our sense of self, even if it means perpetuating a fiction. Despite all we do, however, to build around ourselves the fiction of self, reality will eventually force itself upon us and we will suffer. This doctrine of "no self" is in Buddhism called *anātman*, and it is in many ways the cornerstone on which everything else stands. *Anātman* is the inevitable result of *anitya*.

Important to understanding both *anitya* and *anātman* is the notion of *pratītyasamutpāda*, which is usually translated as "conditioned genesis." The principle of *pratītyasamutpāda* is supplied in a short four-line formula:

> When this is, that is
> This arising, that arises
> When this is not, that is not
> This ceasing, that ceases.

The first of the four premises points to how the conditions of the present moment give rise to the conditions of the next moment. The second premise adds to this by suggesting how the conditions of the present moment, which produce the conditions of the future moment, are themselves the result of conditions of the past moment. Thus the conditions of the past moment give rise to conditions of the future moment, making it impossible to say that the "this" moment of the present ever really exists. There is no moment when one can say the "this" is frozen; there is only "becoming," and this "becoming" is *anitya*. The third and fourth premises are a negation of the first two in that they stop the process of becoming.

A further implication of *pratītyasamutpāda* is that it asserts the interdependent nature of the universe. Any one thing in the universe is connected to and conditioned by all other things. Thus the most ordinary events of the most ordinary day are inextricably linked with events of cosmic significance across the galaxy, and, in the context of *pratītyasamutpāda*, they are no less important. In asserting selfhood, then, one makes two errors. First, one denies the fundamental impermanence of reality; and, second, one looks to remove oneself from being dependent, and thereby allows that the self is the only unconditioned element in the universe.

If the cause of *duḥkha* is thirst, then the cessation of *duḥkha* demands the cessation of thirst, which comprises the third of the Noble Truths. This cessation of *duḥkha* the Buddha calls *Nirvāṇa*, which literally means "to blow out." *Nirvāṇa* is "to blow out" suffering, but this requires that the ignorance that causes this suffering also be blown out. In other words, there must be the cessation of the fiction of the ego self, which leads to the cessation of the thirst for self, which results in the cessation of suffering. Important to remember here are the third and fourth premises which define *pratītyasamutpāda*: "when this is not, that is not; this ceasing, that ceases."

Crucial to this discussion is the Buddhist understanding of rebirth. A question often asked, and not without some justification, is that, if there is no self or no soul, what exactly is reborn. We have already seen one formula that explains the interdependence and relativity of existence. Another formula which explains *pratītyasamutpāda*, only with specific reference to the cycle of human existence, is referred to as the twelve preconditions leading to continued suffering and bondage to rebirth. These conditions, which are very often called the "wheel of life," are as follows:

1. Ignorance
2. Ignorance conditions volitional actions or karmic foundations
3. Volitional actions conditions consciousness
4. Consciousness conditions name and form ("the spark of sentient life")
5. Name and form conditions the six sense fields
6. The six sense fields condition sense contact
7. Sense contact conditions feeling
8. Feeling conditions desire
9. Desire conditions appropriation forces
10. Appropriation forces condition becoming forces
11. Becoming forces condition rebirth
12. Rebirth conditions aging and suffering.

What this formula suggests is that rebirth is the direct product of ignorance. It is not a matter of the soul or self being reborn; rather if one holds on to the fiction of self, which is ignorance, that fiction, given the inevitability of *pratītyasamutpāda* ("when this is, that is"), gives rise to another sentient existence.

   It is sometimes said in regard to the doctrines of *anitya* and *anātman* that Buddhism is a pessimistic religion, espousing what amounts to self-extinction. The fallacy of this argument is that, if there is no self to extinguish, then there can be no self-extinction. But this is really only one answer. Perhaps a better response is to say that a concept such as *anātman* is not a metaphysical concept, and therefore is not something that can be intellectually grasped. In that our thirsts or desires derive from our intellect, then such concepts, in revealing the inadequacy of intellectual reflection, give us a sense of what Buddhism demands of us. Put another way, *anātman*, as well as a concept such as *Nirvāna*, point to an ineffable truth that can be neither thought about nor talked about, and that, as such, is beyond all metaphysical categories. Words used in this way are termed soteriological, which pertains to that dimension of religious expression that motivates and encourages us to pursue liberation or salvation.

It is one thing to say that the cessation of suffering demands the cessation of thirst, but it is quite another to pursue this goal. Knowing this, Śākyamuni supplies the fourth of the Noble Truths: the Path. Usually called the Holy Eightfold Path, the last of the Noble Truths comprises a more specific statement, in terms we can understand, of what it means to rid oneself of thirst. The Holy Eightfold Path is not to be seen as a step by step path towards enlightenment. Rather one must pursue all ideals at the same time: to move closer to realizing one is to move closer to realizing all of them. Finally, the path is a way of perfecting the essentials of Buddhist training: ethical conduct, mental discipline, and wisdom. It is comprised of the following.

1. Right Speech

In the most matter-of-fact terms, Right Speech demands that one abstain from telling lies, from slanderous talk, and from idle gossip. But the meaning of Right Speech encompasses much more than this. Language in large part lies at the root of our problems, for through language we express our mistaken view of ourselves and of reality. Thus Right Speech forces us to reflect on how language deceives us and on how it might be best used to help us achieve the goal of spiritual liberation.

2. Right Action

Demanded here is that one pursue moral conduct, which, for the Buddha, is conduct in which the other is put before the self. If it is the case that egocentricity stands in the way of enlightenment, and that egocentricity is exacerbated by selfish action, then the only way to stop this process is to turn it around by pursuing unselfish actions.

3. Right Livelihood

The Buddha was a practical man, and he knew that people had to make their way in the world. Not everyone, after all, could enter a monastery. Therefore the Buddha directs people to exercise the same principles underlying Right Speech and Right Action in pursuing their particular vocation in life. In the simplest terms, this means one must under no circumstances use people for personal profit or engage in a profession that harms life.

4. Right Effort

This refers to the will to prevent evil and unwholesome thoughts from arising, to get rid of those evil thoughts one already has, and to pursue good thoughts. What is especially important about Right Effort is that it stresses how energy and purposefulness are necessary to spiritual growth.

5. Right Mindfulness or Attentiveness

The Buddha demands that one be keenly sensitive to one's sensations, perceptions, and thoughts. His point is that spiritual growth is only possible if one continuously looks within oneself to discover where one is wanting. Only in this way can one govern one's life accordingly.

6. Right Concentration

Right concentration entails meditational practices that allow one to gain control over those sensations, perceptions, and thoughts that pervert our understanding. In Buddhism, meditation is talked about in any number of ways. One of the most common is the four stages or *dhyāna* of meditation, each of which specifies a particular degree of mental awareness. These stages entail:

1. the removal of unwholesome thoughts and scepticism so that joy and happiness remain.
2. the suppression of intellectual activities and the development of tranquility and "one-pointedness" of mind.
3. the elimination of joy as an active sensation while disposition to happiness remains.

4. the elimination of all disposition leaving full awareness.

Another way of looking at Buddhist meditation is in the context of the "three doors to deliverance,"[2] which are at once the focus and the end of meditation. *Śūnyatā*, or "emptiness," pertains to the state in which one is emptied of all that substantiates selfhood: it is sometimes called "the Void" or the "state of voidness." *Animitta* or "signlessness" refers to the process by which one's mind is turned from the inward calm to the outer world and to how this mental process is to be reversed. Implicit here is the recognition that self is affirmed over against the outer world; thus to disconnect oneself from the outer world is to eliminate the egocenteredness that gives rise to the fiction of self. Finally, *Apraṇihita* or "wishlessness" refers to how grasping after anything perverts our understanding because it presupposes that something can be possessed. To wish for *Nirvāṇa* is, therefore, to push it away, for *Nirvāṇa* is itself a state of "wishlessness."

7. Right Thought

Right Thought requires that one cultivate thoughts of selfless renunciation in one's relationship with other individuals. These thoughts are those that reduce ego centeredness, which is what keeps us fettered to the realm of suffering.

8. Right Understanding

This is *prajñā*: it is the wisdom of seeing things such as they are. Right understanding is not the product of the intellect or of anything that makes us conventionally human. Rather it is a direct apprehension of truth devoid of limitation.

THERAVĀDA METAPHYSICS

Much of the *Abidharma* texts is taken up with the concepts of *anātman* and *anitya*. In this discussion, a central concern is with the continual flow of elements called *dharmas*, which are seen as the fundamental building blocks of reality. Although themselves without spatial and temporal characteristics, the *dharmas*, by virtue of their motions, produce elements and combinations that are both spatial and temporal. The individual or empirical self is nothing more than these impersonal *dharmas*. The word "*dharma*" is thus used in yet another way, albeit in a way still consistent with the meaning "to sustain." *Dharmas* are, very simply, that which sustains or supports reality. But it is understood that these *dharmas* are not absolutes and they have no unconditional reality of their own. Rather the *dharma* of any particular moment is conditioned by what preceded it.

There is suggested in the *Abidharma* discussion of the *dharmas* a twofold perception of change. First, reality, as we know it, and which includes ourselves, is comprised of *dharmas* coming together and dispersing in ever-changing configurations. Second, the *dharmas* are not themselves absolute, and are coming into and going out of existence. It goes without saying that the idea of *dharmas* was the subject of immense conjecture. The *Sarvāstivādins*, for example, talk of the *dharmas* as existing only in the instant of activity but of possessing an "essense" that exists before and after the instant, while another school, the *Śautrāntikas*, saw the *dharmas* as lasting only for one instant, disappearing as soon as they appear.

Another crucial issue for the *Abidharmists* is the nature of the empirical self or the individual. Here they talk about the five "aggregates" or *skandhas*, each comprised of *dharmas*. These *skandhas*, not only account for the existence of the self, but also explain how the self interacts with the external reality. The first *skandha* is form, and includes all those *dharmas* that comprise the material world, as well as our own physical being that interacts with it. The second *skandha* is sensation, which is those *dharmas* that connect our material bodies with a material universe. That each person has a different response to a sensation is explained by the third *skandha*, perception; for example, a similar sensation will for one person register hot and for another cold. It is to be human to respond to our perceptions, and this is accounted for with the fourth *skandha*, mental formations. Included here are involuntary, non-volitional responses such as pulling one's hand away from a hot flame, as well as volitional responses which one "thinks through." After looking at travel literature on Hawaii, for example, one consciously chooses to go on vacation. That the first four *skandhas* work is the result of the fifth *skandha*, consciousness, which serves as a memory bank allowing present experiences to be seen in the context of past experiences. This in turn gives us a sense of self beyond the momentary. At the same time, even consciousness changes, and hence we forget things and see things in new light. What is significant in all this is that nowhere is there a self outside the *skandhas* which exists as the unchanging witness of change.

BUDDHA AND ARHAT

According to *Theravādin* teaching, both the Buddha and the *arhat* are enlightened beings. The difference between the two is, not in the end, but in the means, for both are achieved by overcoming the various fetters confining one to *saṃsāra*. The Buddha is one who has achieved the goal by himself, and in achieving the goal, maps out a path that others can follow. The *arhat* is one who achieves the end by following that path.

While the tendency is to talk about Śākyamuni as "the" Buddha, there are in the *Theravāda* tradition twenty-seven previous Buddhas; the present Buddha, Śākyamuni; and the Buddha to come, Maitreya. The appearance of a Buddha is a very rare event, and the general view is that a Buddha only appears when humankind is so immersed in ignorance that the path to enlightenment has been lost. Some idea of the rarity of the appearance of a Buddha is suggested by the way not every *kalpa* gives rise to one. Thus a distinction is made between "empty" *kalpas* and *kalpas* "blessed with a Buddha." Our *kalpa* is particularly blessed and is termed "the greatly auspicious" *kalpa* of five Buddhas: there have been three Buddhas in the distant past, there is the present Buddha, Śākyamuni, and there is Maitreya, the Buddha "yet to come."

THE MONASTIC ORDER

Theravāda to this day makes a distinction between those belonging to the monastic order and householders. A monastery is called a *sangha*, which referred originally to the Buddhist community generally, but which has taken on the more specific meaning of monastic community. A distinguishing feature of this monastic community is that it admits both men and women (*bhikkhus, bhikkhunis*) in contrast with the Hindu tradition which limits the role of priest to men. One who enters a monastery does so with the intention of making the pursuit of enlightenment the most important goal, and to this end one formally renounces the world in a rite of renunciation. At the same time, however, Śākyamuni specified that there is a crucial reciprocal relationship between members of the monastic order and laypersons. While the monk or nun must serve as a teacher, spiritual guide, and ideal for members of the lay community, the lay community is in return responsible for supplying the material needs of the monks and nuns. A striking expression of this relationship is found in Thailand, Sri Lanka, and Burma, where one can see monks leaving the monastery in the early morning with their alms bowls to gather food. This must not be construed, however, as begging; rather the householder sees it as an obligation to provide the "first fruits" of the table to the monastery, for in so doing one is a good Buddhist and accrues good *karma*.

Entry into the monastery is a two step process.[3] At the age of fifteen, one enters the stage of noviceship, in which one continues until one has achieved sufficient spiritual maturity to become a full member of the order. While a novice, one is under the guidance of a spiritual preceptor and the tutelage of a teacher, both of whom have been full *bhikkhus* or *bhikkunis* for ten years. During this preparatory period, the novice must adhere to the following "Ten Basic Precepts":

1. not to destroy life
2. not to steal
3. not to engage in sexual conduct
4. not to lie
5. not to take alcoholic beverages
6. not to eat at forbidden times (fasts, etc.)
7. not to participate in dancing, singing, etc.
8. not to wear garlands, perfumes, ornaments, etc.
9. not to use high and wide beds
10. not to accept gold or silver.

Once a full member of the order, the monk or nun must adhere to a much longer list of prescriptions found in the *Pātimokkha*, which is one of the most important of the *Vinaya* texts.

Members of the monastic order live a life of rigorous self discipline. They eat only twice a day, and spend long hours in meditation and study of the sacred texts. Monks and nuns give up all their personal possessions when they enter the monastery; all they possess are the distinctive saffron robes they wear. One must not, however, be left with the impression that monks and nuns live out their lives in monastic isolation. Today, for example, they also work in the community as teachers, social workers, agriculturalists, etc.

THE THREEFOLD REFUGE

Regardless of whether one is *Theravāda* or *Mahāyāna*, to be a Buddhist is to take refuge in the three jewels (*Tiratana*): the *Buddha*, the *Dharma*, and the *Sangha*. The Pali word *ratana* points to what brings the highest delight; therefore in the Buddhist context, *ratana* refers to that which brings or induces enlightenment. *Tiratana*, then, is the three things in which one can have refuge and by which one will receive the spiritual strength and resolve necessary to pursue the goal of enlightenment.

For many Buddhists, and especially those not familiar with the scholastic teachings, to have refuge in the Buddha is to give him supernatural powers and to worship him as god. But such a notion of refuge in the Buddha is not quite accurate, even though it brings many people a sense of spiritual satisfaction. To have refuge in the Buddha demands that Śākyamuni remain a man, for it is to identify in him the human embodiment of the realized goal after which all Buddhists quest. The Buddha represents, in other words, the latent potential for enlightenment present within each individual. Thus, having refuge in the Buddha is to see in Śākyamuni a historical example of what can occur for every person, and from this derive the sustaining strength that comes from knowing the goal can be achieved.

To have refuge in the *Dharma* has two meanings, referring at once to what the Buddha said and to what he discovered, although both draw on the basic denotation of "supporting" or "sustaining." In the sense of what the Buddha said, *Dharma* refers to the Four Noble Truths and the Holy Eightfold Path; and to have refuge in the *Dharma* is to accept these teachings as efficacious in leading one to the goal of enlightenment. In the sense of what the Buddha discovered, *Dharma* refers to the ultimate truth and is therefore synonymous with *Nirvāṇa*. Here, to have refuge in the *Dharma* is to believe in the goal, and indeed to accept that it is the highest goal worth pursuing.

Finally, to have refuge in the *sangha* means, in the most general sense, to become part of the Buddhist community and to gain spiritual resolve from sharing a common goal with others. But, as with *Dharma, Sangha* means various things. A second use, as we have seen, is in reference to the monastic order. To have refuge in the *Sangha* is, therefore, to see the monk or nun as a source of particular spirituality as well as a protector of the Dharma, and to accept one's role as a supporter of the monastic order.

THERAVĀDA AND MAHĀYĀNA

The history of *Mahāyāna* is a complex one. It begins with the *Mahāsanghika* sect, which had split away from the more conservative *Sthaviras.* While there were many reasons for this split, the most immediate cause was a concern with the increasing monasticism which the *Mahāsanghikas* identified in the *Sthaviras.* They saw in *Sthaviras* an erosion of the original reciprocal relationship between monk and layperson, as outlined by Śākyamuni, and an increased emphasis by the monk on the goal of personal enlightenment. In this emphasis, the *Mahāsanghikas* identified an ego-centeredness that they felt was contrary to the Buddha's teaching.

As well, there was a concern about the increasing scholasticism characterising many of the Buddhist schools. While the *Sthavira* schools insisted that their teachings were a true account of the Buddha's teachings, and that the *Mahāsanghikas* were at best a liberal splinter group, the *Mahāsanghikas* were themselves concerned that the *Abidharmist* preoccupation with explaining and schematizing was

perverting the basic practicality of the Buddha's
teachings. Here they pointed to the *avyākṛta* or
"inexpressibles," which are specific questions on which
the Buddha is said to have remained silent and which
signal his rejection of metaphysical inquiry:

1. Whether the world is eternal, or not, or
   both, or neither?
2. Whether the world is finite, or infinite, or
   both, or neither?
3. Whether the Tathāgata exists after death,
   or does not, or both, or neither?
4. Is the soul identical with the body or
   different from it?[4]

According to the Buddha, those who pursue such
questions are like the man wounded by an arrow, who
is so concerned with discovering who aimed the arrow,
and from where it came, that he dies. Such enquiries
are in the end harmful and most certainly do not
generate spiritual truth. Thus the criticism was raised
that Buddhism was becoming exactly what the
Buddha rejected, and in the process losing sight of the
basic teaching that it was a means to an end and not
an end in itself.

Between 100 BCE and 100 CE the teachings of
the *Mahāsanghikas* gradually evolved into *Mahāyāna*,
or "great vehicle," which perceived the *Sthaviras* as
Hīnayāna or "small vehicle." The term "*Hīnayāna*" is
intended as a label of criticism, and even today
modern *Theravādins* do not like to be called
Hīnayānists, although scholars tend to use it in a non-
perjorative sense designating the many sects not
Mahāsanghikas that arose between the death of
Śākyamuni and the first century BCE.

THE BODHISATTVA DOCTRINE

It is the general view of *Mahāyāna* that the *arhat* ideal of *Theravāda* is not so much wrong as limited. For *Theravāda*, one who achieves arhatship has achieved enlightenment: there is release from *saṃsāra* and no further rebirth. For *Mahāyāna*, the *arhat* has achieved much in that he has acquired *prajñā* or "wisdom," but this wisdom is not sufficient and must be tempered with compassion if one is to achieve *Nirvāṇa*. One who does so achieves Buddhahood, and thus every individual has the potential to be a Buddha, unlike in *Theravāda* in which there is really only one Buddha and all others who achieve enlightenment are *arhats.*

Crucial to the spiritual process leading to Buddhahood is the path of the *bodhisattva* or "Buddha-to-be," which evolved from the *Mahāyāna* view that the compassion demanded to become a Buddha can only be expressed in helping others achieve the same goal. The *bodhisattva* path leading to Buddhahood is one on which the individual consciously embarks. It is not something done lightly, and requires that one have spent many lifetimes developing *bodhicitta* or the "desire for Buddhahood." Once committed to the path, the *bodhisattva*'s pursuit of wisdom is always tempered by compassion, insofar as both are necessary for the goal to be achieved.

The path of the *bodhisattva* is comprised of ten stages, each marking a stage of increased spiritual awareness.[5] The first stage is that of "joy" (*Pramuditā*), in which the *bodhisattva* experiences the joy of knowing that, because of past actions, it is now possible to embark on the path leading to the goal of enlightenment. The *bodhisattva* is born into the family of the Buddhas, and thereby keeps firmly in mind, "may I become a Buddha to help other creatures achieve enlightenment." The second stage of the path is that of "Immaculate" (*Vimala*), which stresses the practice of morality; in this stage, the *bodhisattva* is said to walk in the Holy Eightfold Path. In the third stage, "Illuminating" (*Prabjakān*), the *bodhisattva* looks to understand the nature of things and expresses patience and forbearance towards those he is committed to helping, while in the fourth stage, "Radiant" (*Archismatī*) the *bodhisattva* strenuously pursues good works, which grow out of the commitment to help others. The fifth stage, "meditation" (*Sadurjayā*) leads directly to the sixth, that of *prajñā* (*Abhimukti*). Crucial here is that this "stage of turning" in *Mahāyāna* is the stage of *arhat* in *Theravāda*. The *bodhisattva*, possessed of wisdom, shines in the "light of *prajñā*."

In *Theravāda*, the goal would now be reached, but not so in *Mahāyāna*, in which there are still four stages to be achieved. At the same time, however, *Mahāyāna* recognizes that the stage of turning is singularly important. Possessed now of *prajñā*, the *bodhisattva* moves where no relative mind can follow. It is conceived that the *bodhisattva*, while remaining in the arena of *saṃsāra*, is elevated to the supramundane state of a "Buddha world" where he continues to pursue his own goal while assisting others achieve theirs. The seventh stage, that of "Far Going" (*Dūrangamā*), is committed to nurturing the skills necessary to lead others to *bodhi*. No longer possessed of worldly thoughts, the *bodhisattva* is committed even more to assisting others suffering in the world.

Accordingly, the *bodhisattva* possesses the ability to take different forms, human or animal, depending on the needs of the sentient creatures requiring help. The eighth stage, that of "Steadfast," entails the possession of the supreme knowledge that lies beyond duality: it is, according to *Mahāyāna* teaching, a knowledge which cannot even be talked about. The mind of the *bodhisattva* is removed from any kind of activity, even though the *bodhisattva* continues to act on behalf of others. Similarly the ninth stage, "The Good" (*Sādhumatī*) and the tenth stage, "The Cloud of the Law" (*Dharmamegha*) are indescribable. In the ninth stage, the *bodhisattva* has all those powers necessary to help all sentient creatures. The tenth stage is that stage at which the *bodhisattva* exhibits the greatest compassion possible in achieving a state of pure egolessness. Having the goal for which he has so long struggled within grasp, the *bodhisattva* turns away from it, committing himself to working for the enlightenment of all other sentient creatures. Thus, in the moment of turning away, the goal is reached.

As well as "the ten stages," the goals of the *bodhisattva* are also defined by the ten *pāramitās* or "perfections," which are best talked about in two groups, the first six, upon which *Mahāyāna* and *Theravāda* agree, and the last four, which belong to *Mahāyāna* alone. The first six *pāramitās* are in many ways a restatement of the Holy Eightfold Path. They include generosity (*Dāna*), morality (*Śīla*), patience (*Kṣānti*), energy (*Vīrya*), contemplation (*Dhyāna*), and wisdom of non-discrimination (*Prajñā*). To these six *pāramitās, Mahāyāna* adds four. The most important of these is the seventh, "skill in means" (*Upāya*), which refers to those means the *bodhisattva* perfects in helping other sentient creatures. The eighth *pāramitā* is resolution (*Praṇidhāna*). This is the resolution needed by the *bodhisattva* to commit himself to helping all other sentient creatures achieve enlightenment. The ninth *pāramitā* is strength (*bala*) necessary to sustaining the other *pāramitās* (patience, will, etc.), and the tenth is transcendental intuition (*jñāna*), which comes from the joining of wisdom and compassion. One way of distinguishing the two groups of *pāramitās*, at least from the *Mahāyāna* perspective, is that the *bodhisattva* pursues the first six as a human being still fettered to relative knowledge, while only the higher-level *bodhisattva*, having achieved *prajñā*, can pursue the final four *pāramitās*. At the same time, however, each of the *pāramitās* is an ideal, and to pursue one *pāramitā* is to pursue all of them. The wisdom and compassion implicit in the *pāramitās* cannot be divorced from one another, and therefore figure in activities of a human, as well as a celestial, *bodhisattva*.

THE DOCTRINE OF THE TRIKĀYA

A second way in which *Theravāda* and *Mahāyāna* differ concerns the concept of the Buddha. While Theravāda recognizes the existence of more than one Buddha, Śākyamuni is, in this historical period, the only one of concern. By contrast, *Mahāyāna* recognizes many Buddhas and *bodhisattvas*, which are said to reside in "Buddha-lands" or "Buddha-worlds." These Buddha-worlds are described using metaphors not unlike those used to describe heaven in the West. Jewels are especially used to describe these paradises, for the imperishability of jewels serves to contrast with the corruption of the organic world.

Explanation of these Buddhas inhabitating Buddha worlds is contained in another fundamental doctrine of *Mahāyāna*, the *Trikāya* or "Three Bodies of the Buddha,"[6] which refers to three different aspects of the Buddha. *Dharmakāya*, or "Body of the Law," is the absolute undifferentiated truth, known variously as the Universal Buddha, *Nirvāna*, *Śūnyatā*, *Tathatā*, etc. *Nirmānakāya*, or "Body of Transformation," is the embodiment of *Dharmakāya* in human form and refers to how the Buddha takes on different manifestations in assisting sentient creatures. Śākyamuni is *Nirmānakāya*: in the way Śākyamuni spoke, in the way he acted, in fact, in everything Śākyamuni did, there is an expression of the absolute truth. *Sāmbhogakāya* or "Body of Enjoyment" is often called the "eternal Buddha" whose body is only enjoyable by higher level *bodhisattvas*. It stands between the undifferentiated suchness of *Dharmakāya* and *Nirmānakāya* that is an expression of *Dharmakāya* in an earthly body.

Sāmbhogakāya is also important for how it gives rise to increasing devotionalism in *Mahāyāna*. *Sāmbhogakāya* is an active force in the world assisting ordinary mortals to achieve enlightenment, and is thereby the focus of devotion and prayer. While technically there is an infinite number of *Sāmbhogakāya*, a select number are especially important. Among these are *Amitābha* or the "Buddha of Infinite Light," who presides over the Buddha-world of *Śukhāvati* or the "western paradise," and *Vairocana* or "Buddha of Illumination," who is sometimes portrayed as the transcendental aspect of Śākyamuni.

Once the Buddha-world and the notion of celestial Buddha were established, there evolved a *Mahāyāna* pantheon which included both Buddhas and *bodhisattvas* arranged in a hierarchy of importance. A few of these *bodhisattvas* also have particular importance. One of the earliest is Maitreya, who, as "the Buddha-of-the future," is technically still a *bodhisattva.* Perhaps the most popular of the *bodhisattvas*, however, is Avalokiteśvara, particularly famous for his "skill in means." Avalokiteśvara is considered the "great helper," and, while originally a male *bodhisattva*, was transformed into a female in China as Kuan Yin. Another significant *bodhisattva* is Mañjuśrī, who is considered the master of *dharma*, and who will, when finally a Buddha, be the "King of *Dharma.*" As master of the *dharma*, Mañjuśrī resides in diverse Buddha-fields sharing his great wisdom with all who desire it.

METAPHYSICAL DIFFERENCES

A third feature distinguishing *Mahāyāna* and *Theravāda* concerns the nature of *śūnyatā* or "voidness." As already discussed, *Theravāda* talks of the *dharmas* as the fundamental units of reality, although it does so in a way which denies them independent reality, making them subject to *pratītyasamutpāda* and possessed of neither temporal nor spatial characteristics. The *Mahāyānists* refused, however, to accept the *Theravādin* view of the *dharmas*, and argued that, no matter what the *Theravādins* said, they could not escape talking about the *dharmas* as if they had some real existence. Thus the *Mahāyānists* see the *dharmas* as just another conventional label that has no reality corresponding to it. They take very seriously the notion of "voidness" as the absence of the duality and polarity characteristic of the intellectual reflection affirming the individual ego.

Two schools of *Mahāyāna* are important for how they address the issue of voidness. *Mādhyamika* or the "middle path" was founded by the notable Indian philosopher Nāgārjuna sometime between 150 and 250 CE. For Nāgārjuna, it is the way we think and express our thoughts in language that lies at the root of our problems. All statements, he argues, express our thirst, not only to define an external reality, but also to affirm our individual existence. Every statement one makes implies individual existence because it suggests an individual who perceives and thinks. To say, for example, "This is a desk" is really to say, "This is a desk for me." Through a form of dialectic called *prasaṅga*, which looks to demonstrate the speciousness of a position without taking another position, Nāgārjuna aims to silence this process and thus point to the voidness that is without discursive thought and beyond expression. The middle position of *Mādhyamika* is one which denies position and suggests the nature of *tathatā* or "suchness." *Tathatā* is without any form of intellectual imposition; thus *Nirvāṇa* is not an alternative reality but is the reality in front of us which we do not see. In the language of *Mādhyamika*, "*Nirvāṇa* is *Saṃsāra* and *Saṃsāra* is *Nirvāṇa*."

A second school of *Mahāyāna* that treats the matter of *śūnyatā* is *Yogācāra* ("practice of yoga"). Largely the product of the two brothers, Asaṅga and Vasubandhu, in the third century CE, *Yogācāra* denies the existence of any kind of external reality. Because what we see and perceive cannot be seen and perceived without consciousness, *Yogācāra* claims the only thing of which one can be certain is consciousness. From this, *Yogācāra* insists that what we perceive as an external reality is the result of concepts imposed by the mind subject to the limitations of ignorance. Thus what is necessary is that through *yoga* this process of the mind be silenced so that uninhibited consciousness or "voidness" remains.

LATER DEVELOPMENTS

To limit any discussion of Buddhism to a consideration of its Indian developments is to do the tradition a severe injustice. Yet limitations of space demand only a very brief treatment of Buddhism as it is found in South East Asia, China, Tibet, Korea, and Japan, even though much of the richness of Buddhism comes from developments outside India.

The growth of Buddhism in India is directly tied to one man, the emperor Aśoka, who was the first ruler to control most of the Indian subcontinent. The final holdout to the suzerainty of Aśoka was the area of Kaliṇga in northeast India, which he overcame in 260 BCE with great violence and bloodshed. Aśoka was apparently so filled with remorse that he turned to study Buddhism as a layperson, and five years later initiated the policy known as "*Dharma*-conquest," by which he had a series of Buddhist edicts engraved on rocks throughout the empire. It was under Aśoka that Buddhism, along with Indian culture generally, spread outside India, in particular to Ceylon and South East Asia. It is generally held that Aśoka sent both religious and political envoys as far as Syria and Egypt.

By the turn of the common era, however, Buddhism was on the decline in India, and, by the sixth century CE, Buddhism had almost disappeared from India, and China had become the new center of Buddhism. One can point to a number of reasons for this decline. First, a form of religious expression known as Tantra crept into Buddhism, and, as Tantric elements also figured prominently in Hinduism, it became difficult to determine where Buddhism ended and Hinduism began. Second, Buddhism exercised extreme tolerance towards other religions, given its view that the path to wisdom is different for different persons. Such tolerance also clouded the distinction between Hinduism and Buddhism. Third, the devotionalism of theistic Hinduism, and especially Śaivism and Vaiṣṇavism, became immensely popular. Appealing to the ordinary person on a very basic emotional level, it stood in striking contrast to the growing conservatism of Buddhism and its increasing emphasis on the monastic order. Finally, the Muslim invasion in the sixth century swept aside everything in its path, whether Hindu or Buddhist, and in particular wiped out the great monasteries at Gandhāra in northwest India.

SRI LANKA AND S.E. ASIA

Buddhism is said to have moved into Sri Lanka (Ceylon) in 256 BCE when Aśoka sent his "Dharma-envoys" at the request of the island's ruler. Initially, Buddhism in Ceylon was associated only with the ruling class, and this relationship has in fact continued to the present day, although gradually Buddhism has filtered down to the ordinary people. The Buddhism of Sri Lanka is *Theravāda*, and, while *Mahāyāna* made some advances in the third and fourth centuries, the country has remained largely *Theravāda* to the present time.

Buddhism also moved into Southeast Asia through the efforts of Aśoka, and, by the end of the second century CE, Burma, Cambodia, and Laos had become centers for a flourishing Buddhist culture. Thailand is today the most important centre of *Theravāda*, and, although much of the original teaching has remained unchanged, Thai Buddhism is very distinctive, fusing as it has with much of the popular religion of the area, which recognizes a whole array of good and bad spirits. This assimilation of localized indigenous beliefs into the larger Buddhist structure is especially noticeable in rural areas, where the people are much more sensitive to the benevolent and benign forces of nature and are to a certain extent uncontaminated by urban cosmopolitanism.

The centre of Thai Buddhism is the *wad* or temple-monastery complex, where the traditional relationship between monastic order and lay order continues. As of 1975, there were some 120,000 monks and nuns in Thai monasteries. While in earlier times, men and women joined the monastery as a lifetime commitment, monasteries today are also looked upon as spiritual retreats. Young boys will enter the monastery as part of their formal education, and adults will live as novices for a time as a means of spiritually rejuvenating themselves and getting back in touch with their own tradition.

CHINA

The development of Chinese Buddhism is an immensely complex affair, as it joined Indian Buddhism with such indigenous Chinese traditions as Taoism and Confucianism, as well as with an amalgam of beliefs and practices generally termed popular Chinese religion. While historical records for the period are suspect, the *Pien-cheng-lun* (*On the Discussion of the Correct*) documents a steady growth in numbers of Buddhist nuns and monks, as well as temples, during the Eastern Chin Dynasty (317-420) and the Northern Wei Dynasty (356-534).[7] By the sixth century, Buddhism was established as a dominant religious force in China, and, while it was not immune from periodic persecution, Buddhism became a distinctly Chinese religion with the development of specific Chinese schools in the seventh and eighth centuries. There are a number of reasons why Buddhism found a home in China. Most obvious of these is that the indigenous religious philosophy of Taoism possessed a number of similarities with Buddhism, and therefore provided a sympathetic home for Buddhist ideas. Beyond this, one can point to the serious political and moral disintegration of China at the end of the Han Dynasty in the second century CE, and how Buddhism provided an alternative to traditions that did not seem able to answer the problems of the day. Buddhism offered a new way of looking at the individual and the world in place of a stale Confucianism that stressed ritual and social relationships.

The most significant event in the development of Buddhism in China was the translation of Indian Buddhist texts into Chinese. The Chinese did not possess a language which could fully translate the Sanskrit originals, but there was in China the indigeneous philosophical-religious system of Taoism, which had an appearance of similarity with Indian Buddhism, and which therefore supplied much of the language needed to talk about Buddhist ideas. The result of this is that Buddhism took on a distinctively Chinese character, in some respects quite different from its Indian origin. Among the many translaters of Buddhist texts, by far the most important was the Indian monk Kumarajīva (344-413), who was a crucial figure in the spreading of *Mādhyamika* into China.

Of the important Chinese schools, two of them, *Ch'an* and Pureland, will be left for discussion in their Japanese context, albeit they are really Chinese developments. A third school, *T'ien T'ai* is important, not so much for introducing new teachings, as for adding a dimension of order to the scattered and often contradictory Buddhist teachings coming into China from India. Beginning with Hui-ssu (515-576) and later developed by his disciple, Chih-i (538-579), who is considered the tradition's great master, *T'ien T'ai* is a school of systematization that puts the sūtras into an order that reflects the audience to whom the Buddha was preaching. Important among *T'ien T'ai*'s teachings is that of "the five periods," which refers to specific periods of the Buddha's life during which he preached.[8]   The first of these is the *Hua-yen* (*Avataṃsaka*) during which the Buddha is said to have preached the *Avataṃsaka Sūtra*. Unfortunately, few could understand the sublime teachings of this sūtra, and therefore the Buddha had recourse to teach in a second period called *A-han (Āgamas)* the more readily understandable ideas of the *Nikāyas*, although he fully understood that they were accommodations of ideas far more sophisticated in their scope and significance. The teachings of this second period included the Four Noble Truths and the Holy Eightfold Path. While the *Hua-yen* lasted only three weeks, the *A-han* lasted twelve years. The period of the *A-han* was itself preparatory to *Fang-teng* (*Vaipulya*) in which the Buddha preached over eight years the superiority of the *Mahāyāna* doctrine, although revealing the full significance of *Mahāyāna* had to wait for the next period, the *Ta-pan-jo* (*Mahāprajñāpāramitā*), which lasted twenty-two years. Finally, the Buddha felt humankind was ready for the highest teachings of the *Saddharma Puṇḍarīka*, which he preached over eight years in the period of the *Fa-hua nieh-p'an*.

Not everything, however, was smooth going in China, and Buddhism faced a significant challenge in Confucianism, which, among other things, underpinned a highly formalized, highly ritualized state government in which both individuals and organizations had rigorously defined responsibilities and roles. The notion of a monastic order answerable only to itself was, not only foreign to Confucian thinking, but an invitation for social and political anarchy. While it is impossible to generalize for all parts of China, Buddhism eventually came under direct government control, as the number of monks and nuns was rigorously limited, the argument being that too many individuals in the monasteries took away valuable human resources needed for the smooth running of society. The monasteries were not, moreover, entirely blameless. In the highly regulated Chinese society, the monastery gradually took on many of the trappings of a political organization rather than a religious one, acquiring immense wealth as well as social and

political influence.   It is hardly surprising that those
in power looked to control this growing Buddhist
influence.

Ironically, though, the great threat to Buddhism
in China did not come from the Confucianists but
from   the   Taoists,   who   might   have   possessed   a
worldview similar to the Buddhists, but who also
aspired to political influence at court.   In 845, in
what is known as the "Great T'ang Persecution," the
emperor, at the instigation of the Taoists, decreed the
destruction of all but a few Buddhist temples,
confiscated all Buddha images for their metal, returned
the monks and nuns to lay life, and took over the
monastic lands.   The next emperor, it is true, reversed
the policy of his predecessor, allowing the reinstitution
of Buddhism, but never again was Buddhism to
achieve its previous glory in China. Buddhism
continued, and indeed grew over the next thousand
years or so, but it never seriously challenged the
dominant Confucian ideology and in many respects
ceased to be either an intellectual or a religious
stimulus in China. With the Cultural Revolution of
the 1950s, however, Buddhism suffered again from
wholescale persecution, and, while the present
Communist Chinese government has allowed some
temples to reopen, one is tempted to see such activity
as having much to do with politics and little to do
with religion.

TIBET

Buddhism in Tibet, and today as it is practiced
in Nepal, stands in some ways quite apart from other
forms of Buddhism. The history of Buddhism in Tibet

can be traced back to at least the eighth century, when, as a result of the Tibetan military takeover of Chinese territory, Tibetan scholars came into contact with their Chinese counterparts and with Chinese Buddhism. At the same time, there was considerable interaction between Tibet and India, and thus Indian Buddhism also found its way into Tibet. Both forms of Buddhism, moreover, interacted with the indigenous religions of Tibet, and this has made Tibetan Buddhism particularly distinctive. This is not to say that Tibetan Buddhism is reduced to an undisciplined syncretism, for, as more than one commentator has observed, Tibetan Buddhism must be seen as an accretion of earlier Buddhist schools that is at once devotional, meditational, and philosophical.

Tibetan Buddhism is dominated by *Tantrayāna*,[9] or the path of *Tantra*, which is not so much a philosophical school as a practical method. A major feature of *Tantra* is its approach to the human body, which most other forms of Buddhism see as a detriment to achieving enlightenment, but which *Tantra* views as a vehicle or vessel of enlightenment. Concomitant with this view of the body is the notion that the world is not so much a hindrance to enlightenment as a source. Thus *Tantra* demands that one work to recognize everything in the world, not as voidness but as fullness, and as being pregnant with the beauty of pure wisdom. To this end, one must approach every sound as having the capacity to open one's minds to this fullness, and every person possessing the capacity to be a Buddha.

In this reliance on the body, Tantric conduct entails three things. "Vanquishing" is the ideal, entailing the vanquishing of desire even while faced

with it. Thus one interacts with the world, but is
never consumed by it. Second is "Ennobling," in
which one transfers the force of one's passions to
mental symbols that encourage an opening of the
mind. Important in this regard is the maṇḍala, which
is a complex of symbols said to comprise a portal to
ultimate reality. Finally, there is "Yielding," which
actually contains two possibilities. The first is to yield
to temptation while maintaining one's attention at all
times on the consequences of one's actions. As one
comes to see that the rewards of giving in to
temptation are poor, one will ultimately experience the
dissipation of desire or thirst. A second way is the
"difficult path" for the very few, in which one, while
participating in the act, transfers all one's human
urges to the urge for liberation. During sexual
intercourse, therefore, one will withdraw one's mind
from the act itself and direct one's energies towards
liberation.

Today the state of Buddhism in Tibet is
unclear, given the continued presence of the Chinese.
Tibetan Buddhism has, however, continued to thrive
in Nepal. There are essentially two major groups in
Tibetan Buddhism. The *Nyingmapas* or "Red Hats"
are the oldest, tracing their lineage back to the great
scholar Padma Sambhava, who is said to have reached
Tibet in 745. He is recognized as Guru Rimpoche or
the "Precious Teacher." The *Gelugpas* or Yellow Hats
go back as far as Atisa, and differ from the
Nyingmapas in encouraging monastic life. While the
lamas or *gurus* of the *Nyingmapas* marry and have
families, the *Gelugpas* espouse discipline and celibacy.
Since 1640, the Dalai Lama, who comes from the
Gelugpas, has been the religious and secular head of
Tibet, even while today he lives in exile in northern
India.

KOREA

According to tradition, Buddhism was brought to northern Korea in 372 CE by the Chinese monk Shun-tao and in a relatively short period of time spread throughout Korea. For all intents and purposes, Korean Buddhism is Chinese Buddhism, and even today Korean monks read the sūtras in Chinese. The history of Buddhism in Korea has clearly been up and down. The seventh to the eleventh centuries stands as the golden period for Buddhism in Korea, but this Buddhist domination was replaced by a rigid Confucianism culminating in the sixteenth century with severe suppression that entailed the numbering of Buddhist sects and the closing of the monasteries. It was not, in fact, until the turn of the twentieth century that Buddhism enjoyed any kind of revival in Korea. This revival continues unabated to this day in South Korea, where there remains but one sect of Buddhism. Given the Communist domination of North Korea, the future of Buddhism there remains unclear.

JAPAN

Buddhism came into Japan through Korea. This early Buddhism is explicitly Chinese, and, for a very long time, Japanese Buddhism was simply Chinese Buddhism filtered through Korea. The actual story of how Buddhism came into Japan is an interesting one, although one is not sure how much is apocraphal and how much historical. It is said that, during the last half of the sixth century, Korean kings

sent various Buddha images to Japan, along with a
message extolling the wisdom of Buddhism. Initially
the Japanese thought there would be no harm in
worshipping these new deities, and, in fact, some good
might come of it. But when a plague broke out, the
Japanese emperor concluded that the indigenous
Shintō deities were offended and had the images
dumped in a moat and the first temple destroyed. A
second plague produced the same result. But, when
the plague carried on, the Buddha images were
retrieved. Miraculously the plague ended and
Buddhism was in Japan to stay.

There are many Japanese contributions to
Buddhism worthy of mention. Perhaps most familiar
to westerners is Zen, which originated with the
Chinese school of *Ch'an*. While coming to Japan in
the eighth century, it did not take on anything
distinctively Japanese until the time of the Zen
teacher, Eisai (1141-1215), himself a former *Tendai*
monk (*T'ien T'ai*). One of the most popular forms of
Buddhism in Japan is Pureland, which really has two
forms *Jōdo-shu* (Pureland sect), initiated by Hōnen
(1133-1212), and *Jōdo-shin-shu* (True Pureland sect),
established by Shinran (who was one of Hōnen's
disciples). A third popular school is *Nichiren*, founded
by the man Nichiren (1222-1282), who took a
decidedly polemical view towards other forms of
Buddhism.

Zen comes from the Japanese word *zenna*
meaning meditation. A monastic form of Buddhism,
monks practice *zazen* or "sitting meditation." Zen
may well be seen as a culmination of *Mādhyamika* and
Yogācāra insofar as it presents *Nirvāṇa* or *Satori*, as
Zen calls it, as an immediate insight into the truth of

reality in which conventional understanding is revealed to be empty. Most daring here is the Zen notion of *koan*, which is a nonsense statement on which the Zen monk will meditate in an attempt to break down the intellectual fictions with which we surround ourselves. One of the most famous koans is "what is the sound of one hand clapping?" The *koan* is really just a combination of words, all of which we recognize and which have meaning for us. When we put them together, however, the statement makes no sense: there is no external reality to correspond to the sound of one hand clapping. The Zen point is that all statements we make are no different than the obvious nonsense of the *koan*: we just simply refuse to see what is there.

In Pureland Buddhism, regardless of whether it is *Jōdo-shu* or *Jōdo-shin-shu*, the focus of devotion is the Amida Buddha, who, in his eighteenth vow as recounted in the *Sukhāvatī-Vyūha-Sūtra*, commits himself to working for the enlightenment of all sentient creatures. Pureland makes a distinction between *shōdo* or the "holy path" and *jōdo* or the "Pureland Path." The holy path is that of the *bodhisattva*, which Hōnen, while seeing as appropriate for the few, felt was out of reach for the majority of people: it is, very simply, too difficult. Thus there is another path, that of *jōdo*. Here Hōnen makes another distinction between *jiriki*, or dependence on self, and *tariki*, or dependence on the other. *Jiriki* corresponds with *shōdo* or the *bodhisattva* path: to achieve enlightenment this way is to rely exclusively upon one's own energies. *Jōdo* is *tariki* in the sense of being reliant upon the immense compassion of the Amida. *Tariki* in Pureland requires that one repeat the name of the Amida in the true belief that he will extend sufficient compassion towards one to guarantee *Nirvāṇa*. The so-called *nembutsu* (shortened form of *Namu Amida Butsu*) is one of the most distinguishing features of Pureland Buddhism, repeated constantly when the devotee goes to the temple. *"Namu"* refers to the act of surrender and *"Amida Butsu"* to the "Buddha of Infinite Light."

While *Jōdo-shu* and *Jōdo-shin-shu* agree on the efficacy of faith and total reliance on Amida, there are very definite differences. Hōnen insisted on numerous repetitions of the *nembutsu* to confirm one's dependence on Amida, while Shinran felt the repetition of the *nembutsu* once in true faith is sufficient and all other repetitions are simply expressions of gratitude. A second distinction focuses on the concept of *Sukhāvatī*, which in the *Sukhāvatī-Vyūha-Sūtra* is described as the Buddha-world of Amida. In *Jōdo*, the view is that sincere repetition of the *nembutsu* guarantees rebirth in *Sukhāvatī* or the "Land of Purity," where conditions are so propitious that enlightenment is guaranteed. The thinking here is that the mundane world is simply too corrupt for the individual to jump straight to enlightenment. By contrast, *Jōdo-shin-shu* sees *Sukhāvatī* as a metaphoric expression for *Nirvāṇa*, having no independent reality of its own.

A distinctly Japanese school is *Nichiren*. The story of this school is that Nichiren the boy entered the monastery on Mount Hiei, but soon became dissatisfied with the inadequacies of its teachings and the general corruption of the monastic order. Going back to the *Lotus Sūtra*, he became convinced that chanting the "Salutation to the *Lotus Sūtra*" (*Namu-myo-ho-ren-ge-kyo*) was sufficient to bring enlightenment. According to Nichiren, anyone who pronounced the salutation would become a Buddha. Nichiren came to see himself as the last incarnation of the Buddha, and, as such, saw as his mission the purifying of Buddhism. To this end, he was highly critical of other forms of Buddhism, particularly *Shingon*, Zen and Pureland. Although exiled on several occasions, his vision of making Japan a Buddha-world on earth was one which had tremendous appeal and attracted many followers.

CONCLUSION

Buddhism is still largely a religion of the east, although one cannot help but notice the proliferation of Buddhist congregations in North America. The majority of these are Japanese and draw from the descendents of Japanese immigrants. Called the Buddhist Churches of America, these congregations, while following *Jōdo-shin-shu* teachings, have adjusted to the western Protestant model of ministers and Sunday worship services. Another large group of Buddhists are Caucasians, who first came into contact with Buddhism as part of the counterculture movement of the 1960s, when young people were looking for alternatives to the lifestyles of their parents. This group is heavily influenced by Zen, and is structured around the practice of meditation. Recently, with the immigration of Vietnamese and Tibetans to North America, there has developed a third group, which has also attracted a following among native-born Canadians and Americans.

Buddhism, as a mental discipline and a perspective on life, has also had a significant impact

in North America. Popularizers such as Alan Watts
have identified in Buddhism an antitode for the stress
and anxiety symptomatic of contemporary life. Thus
people have been drawn to Buddhism, not as a
religion, but as a way of freeing oneself from the
preoccupations of western materialism. There is little
question that Buddhism's emphasis on tolerance and
compassion, and its focus on the individual, have
proven very appealing to non-Asiatics of all sorts.
Despite Buddhism's incredibly rich scholastic tradition,
which has produced all variety of Buddhist expression,
there is a deep-seated unity in Buddhism that is
immensely satisfying and that makes Buddhism a
powerful alternative to the dogmatism, religious or
otherwise, that espouses exclusivity and absoluteness of
truth.

Notes

[1]I am much indebted in my discussion of the
Four Noble Truths to Walpola Rahula, *What The
Buddha Taught*, 2nd edition (1959; rpt. New York:
Grove Press, 1974).

[2]For more extensive discussion, see Edward
Conze, *Buddhist Thought in India* (1962; rpt. Ann
Arbor: The University of Michigan Press, 1982), pp.
59-69.

[3]See Robert Lester, *Theravada Buddhism in
Southeast Asia* (Ann Arbor: The University of
Michigan, 1973) for discussion of sangha organization
and the Threefold Refuge.

[4]Quoted in T.R.V. Murti, *The Central
Philosophy of Buddhism* (1955; rpt. London: Unwin
Paperbacks, 1980), p. 38.

[5]My discussion draws on Beatrice Lane Suzuki, *Mahāyāna Buddhism* (1969; rpt. New York: Macmillan, 1972), pp. 65-74.

[6]See Ibid., pp. 52-62.

[7]Richard H. Robinson, Willard L. Johnson, *The Buddhist Religion*, 3rd edition (1970; rpt. Belmont: Wadsworth Publishing, 1982), pp. 188-189.

[8]See Kenneth Ch'en, *Buddhism in China* (1964; rpt. Princeton: Princeton University Press, 1973), pp. 305-311.

[9]I draw here on Bhikshu Sangharakshita, *A Survey of Buddhism* (Boulder: Shambhala, 1980), pp. 368-390.

Selected Readings

Bond, George D. *The World of the Buddha.* Colombo, Sri Lanka: M.D. Gunasena and Company, 1982.

Blofeld, John. *The Tantric Mysticism of Tibet.* Boulder: Prajna Press, 1982.

Carter, John Ross. *The Threefold Refuge in the Theravāda Buddhist Tradition.* Pennsylvania: Anima Publications, 1982.

Conze, Edward. *Buddhist Scriptures.* Baltimore: Penguin Books, 1959.

Dumoulin, Heinrich. *The History of Zen Buddhism.* Trans. Paul Peachey. Boston: Beacon Press, 1963.

Dutt, Ramesh C. *Buddhism and Buddhist Civilization in India.* Delhi: Seema Publications, 1983.

Hopkins, Jeffrey. *Meditation on Emptiness.* London: Wisdom Publications, 1983.

Jacobson, Nolan Pliny. *Buddhism and the Contemporary World.* Illinois: Southern Illinois University Press, 1983.

Kawamura, Leslie S. (ed.) *The Bodhisattva Doctrine in Buddhism.* Waterloo: Wilfred Laurier University Press, 1981.

Ling, Trevor. *The Buddha.* Harmondsworth: Penguin, 1976.

Mizuno, Kogen. *Buddhist Sūtras: Origin, Development, and Transmission.* Tokyo: Kosei Publishing, 1982.

Murti, T.R.V. *The Central Philosophy of Buddhism,* 2nd. ed., 1955; rpt. London: Unwin Paperbacks, 1980.

Paul, Diana Y. *Women in Buddhism.* Berkeley: Asian Humanities Press, 1979.

Picken, Stuart D.B. *Buddhism: Japan's Cultural Identity.* San Francisco: Kodansha International, 1982.

Rahula, Walpola. *What the Buddha Taught.* Surrey: Unwin Brothers, 1972.

Ramanan, K. Venkata. *Nāgārjuna's Philosophy.* Delhi: Motilal Banarsidass, 1978.

Reischauer, August Karl. *Studies in Japanese Buddhism.* New York: The Macmillan Company, 1917.

Robinson, Richard H. and Willard R. Johnson. *The Buddhist Religion*, 3rd ed., 1970; rpt. Belmont, California: Wadsworth Publishing, 1982.

Sangharakshita, Bhiksu. *A Survey of Buddhism*. Boulder: Shambhala Publications, 1980.

Snellgrove, David and Hugh Richardson. *A Cultural History of Tibet*. New York: Praegan, 1968.

Suzuki, Beatrice Lane. *Mahāyāna Buddhism*. New York: The Macmillan Company, 1969.

Suzuki, D.T. *Zen Buddhism: Selected Writings of D.T. Suzuki*. Ed. William Barrett. New York: Doubleday and Company, 1956.

Stryk, Lucien (ed.) *World of the Buddha: A Reader*. New York: Doubleday and Company, 1969.

Toshihiko, Izutsu. *Towards a Philosophy of Zen Buddhism*. Boulder: Prajna Press, 1982.

Wright, Arthur F. *Buddhism in Chinese History*. Stanford, California: Stanford University Press, 1959.

Yoshinori, Takeuchi. *The Heart of Buddhism*. Trans. James W. Heisig. New York: Crossroad Publishing, 1983.

Yu, Lu K'uan. *Ch'an and Zen Teaching*. Berkeley: Shambhala Publications, 1970.

CHAPTER IV

THE RELIGIONS OF CHINA AND JAPAN

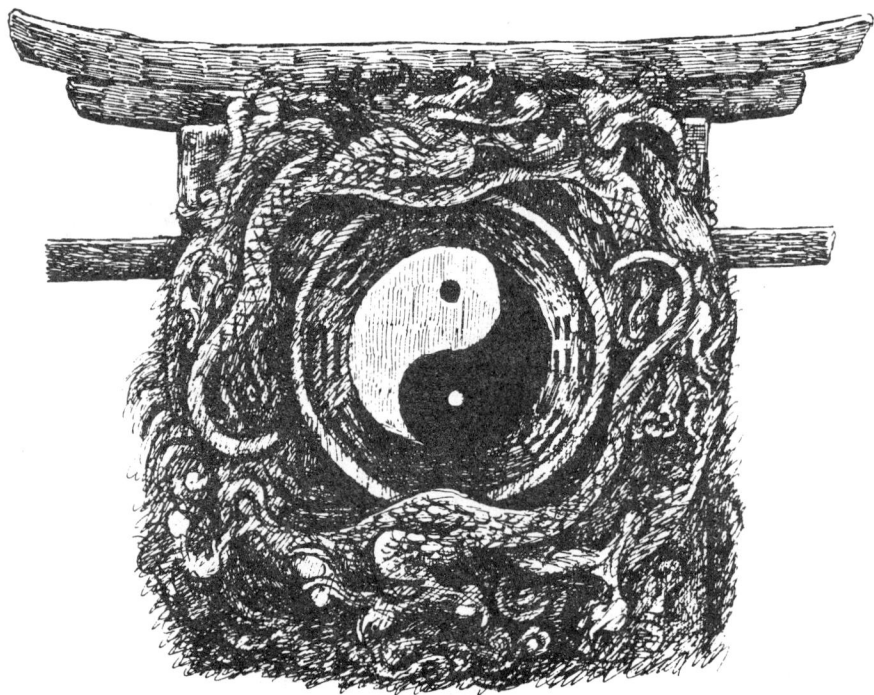

IV

THE RELIGIONS OF CHINA
AND JAPAN

INTRODUCTION

It may perhaps seem incongruous and a bit misleading to place in a single chapter the religions of China and Japan. Yet there is a distinctively east-Asian view of things that largely remains constant in the indigenous traditions of China and Japan. This east-Asian attitude is most obviously expressed in a spiritual orientation towards this world rather than towards the next. While concern with the "wholly other" is most certainly present in these religions, the experience of this "other" is one which leads to a better and happier life now: whatever radical transformation takes place in the individual has consequences for the present, and there is little, if any, concern about what happens later, either in this life or in a life after death.

Pervasive, as well, is the recognition of a divine order or way, of which humankind is a part. Unfortunately, we choose to separate ourselves from this crder or way to see ourselves as possessing special status in the universe. We do this, moreover, even though all evidence points to how we are wrong: immersed in self-imposed ignorance, we suffer a sense of incompleteness and anxiety because we cannot accept the true nature of things. Thus the aim of east-Asian religions is to integrate the individual back into the divine order, and in this regard the natural world looms large as an expression of the harmony in which we must willingly participate. Finally, the religions of China and Japan are distinctive in that they cannot be separated off from the rest of life. Not only does this make difficult the identification of what is specifically religious, but it also contributes to how these traditions intimately touch the lives of people in ways that might not always be identified as religious.

THE CHINESE CONTEXT

When one first approaches Chinese religions, one is confronted by two problems. First, textbooks dealing with Chinese religions usually dwell on two forms of religious expression, Taoism and Confucianism. If one goes to China, however, one would be hardpressed to find a practising Taoist or

Confucianist. A second problem is that Chinese popular religion, as found in the many temples of Hong Kong, Taiwan, and Macau, seems to bear no relationship to the more "philosophical" expressions of Chinese religion; in fact, to the outsider, popular Chinese religion seems an eclectic collection of spirit worship, geomancy, ancestor worship, and fortune telling. We have seen elsewhere that the popular expression of a religious tradition and the philosophical-scholastic expression of a tradition sometimes diverge, but always there is maintained the relationship that one is a living expression of what the other intellectually explains and justifies. In Chinese religions, however, this relationship seems absent.

Taoism and Confucianism, which together comprise the major religious-philosophical streams of China, grew out of a common political and social environment. Little is known of Chinese history prior to the establishment of the Hsia dynasty (c.2205 BCE), and, even the Hsia dynasty, as well as the following Shang Dynasty (c.1766-c.1122), remain vague and ill-defined. Chinese history begins proper with the Chou Dynasty (1122-256 BCE), during which much of China was consolidated. In the eighth century BCE, however, there was considerable turmoil within the Chou empire, the result being a split into the Western Chou and the Eastern Chou. The Eastern Chou was in turn made up of a number of states with expansionist ideas, which were constantly at each other's throats. This period in Chinese history is known as that of the Spring and Autumn and the Warring States. As a period of political, social, and moral disorder, it comprised a period of real crisis for the Chinese, who had for centuries considered themselves possessed of the world's greatest

civilization, and viewed people outside their borders as
"barbarians." In response to the chaos of the period,
a number of thinkers emerged who sought to find a
solution to China's problems, and who, in doing so,
examined some of the very basic issues facing
humankind. It was out of this intellectual ferment
that came the two great traditions, Taoism and
Confucianism, which, while addressing the same
problems, looked at the world and humankind's place
in it very differently.

TAOISM

According to legend, Lao-tzu (Master Lao) was
the originator of Taoism. We know virtually nothing
about Lao-tzu, except that he is purported to have
composed a book, the *Tao Te Ching* (*The Way and
its Power*), which remains one of the great religious
and philosophical documents of all time.
Traditionally, Lao-tzu is said to have lived in the
sixth century BCE, but scholars now place the *Tao
Te Ching* about three centuries later. A second
important individual in Taoism is Chuang-tzu, who is
placed at the end of the fourth century BCE, although
this too is questionable. Chuang-tzu produced a
remarkable philosophical work which to this day
remains nameless; therefore, convention has it that the
work produced by Chuang-tzu is called the
Chuang-tzu.

Crucial to an understanding of Taoism is the
word "*Tao*," meaning "road" or "way," which is one
of the most important terms in Chinese philosophical
language, used by many thinkers in addition to Lao-
tzu and Chuang-tzu. In Taoism, however, the word

"*Tao*," takes on a very specific meaning. *Tao* is the first principle from which all things come. It is the unnameable, indescribable, and unknowable. As Lao-tzu says, "there was something undifferentiated yet complete . . . soundless and formless, it depends on nothing and does not change. It operates everywhere and is free from danger. It may be considered the mother of the universe. I do not know its name, I call it *Tao*."[1] But *Tao* is also more than this. *Tao* refers to all that comes from the first principle; if *Tao* is non-being, it is also being, and thereby involves efficiency and power. This form of *Tao* is termed *Te* or the "ten thousand things," and is seen as *Tao* in form. Thus Lao-tzu writes, "*Te* is the dwelling place of *Tao*. Things obtain it [from *Tao*] so as to be produced. Living things obtain it so as to function; it is the essence of *Tao*."[2]

Finally, there is a third dimension of *Tao*, which pertains to the process by which the unnameable becomes the nameable. Here Taoism draws on two additional concepts, the *yin* and the *yang*, which represent in Chinese thinking the polar reality of the universe. In Taoism, the universe evolves because of the interaction of opposites. The Taoist sees that there cannot be hot without cold, high without low, rich without poor, happiness without sorrow, or life without death. Very often the *yang* is associated with the negative or active male principle and the *yin* with the positive or passive female principle. The particulars of *yin* and *yang*, however, do not matter. What does matter is *hsiang sheng* or "mutual arising." That opposites exist means that the universe exists because it is the interaction of these opposites that produce the universe; or, as Lao-tzu writes:

Tao produced the One
The one produced the two.
The two produced the three.
And the three produced the ten thousand
things.
The ten thousand things carry the *yin* and
embrace the *yang* and through the blending of
the material force they achieve harmony.[3]

One can conclude, then, that all is *Tao*, given that
the *Tao* is at once the first principle from which all
things come and to which all things return, all those
things which come from this first principle, and the
process by which the unformed takes form.

If everything is *Tao*, how exactly can this Tao
be described? Here Lao-tzu and Chuang-tzu are
reluctant to comment, although they do say two very
crucial things. First *Tao* is described as ever-changing:
the process by which the unformed becomes the
formed is one in which nothing remains the same from
one moment to another. Second, *Tao* is said to be
spontaneous: "the Great Tao flows everywhere. / It
may go left or right."[4] The *Tao* is not something
that is planned: it cannot be anticipated or explained.
Thus in Taoism it is usual to explain things as
happening because it is the way of the *Tao*.

The spiritual goal in Taoism is to achieve the
sage's perspective of nonintervention or *wu wei*. In
that there is nothing that one can do to influence the
Tao, one must learn to govern one's life in accordance
with the *Tao*. While the inanimate universe operates
without awareness, and lower animate creatures
operate according to instinct, the human being
possesses self-awareness, and in Taoism is therefore
talked about as the *Tao* being conscious of itself.

Possessing self-consciousness, the individual seems to have some control over his life. It is here that one makes a crucial mistake. One inevitably thinks one can remake the universe according to one's own plan, and, while for a time one might seem to be successful, the reality that one is simply part of the vastness of the *Tao* will inevitably come crashing into one's make-believe world. Therefore, what the individual must do is come to understand the nature of the *Tao*, and accept that what one is and what one does are part of this great cosmic force. Only when the individual does so will he be free from frustration and suffering.

One must see things from the standpoint of the *Tao*. Behind the notion of *wu wei* is the view that everything in nature comes about of itself, without any particular kind of intervention. *Wu wei* is, therefore, natural, spontaneous action performed in an effortless state of mind. Of course, this is easier said than done, and neither Lao-tzu nor Chuang-tzu are forthcoming with specific advice. For them to give advice would be to impose human conventions on natural process, which is the very thing which cannot be done. There is, however, one fundamental principle which suggests what *wu wei* entails. This single principle is that whatever life style one lives, one must also live its opposite. This is Lao-tzu's message when he says:

To yield is to be preserved whole.
To be bent is to become straight.
To be empty is to be full.
To be worn out is to be renewed.
To have little is to possess.
To have plenty is to be perplexed.
Therefore the sage embraces the One

And becomes the model of the world.[5]

Crucial to what Lao-tzu refers here is the Taoist
assertion that through the interaction of opposites the
universe evolves. Each of us is, however, reluctant to
accept this fundamental nature of the universe. One
might recognize that one cannot have youth without
old age, beauty without ugliness, health without
sickness, wealth without poverty, life without death,
but one still hangs on to one or other of the items
comprising a pair, and in the process makes a value
judgment: beauty is better than ugliness, health better
than sickness, life better than death. But such is not
the way of things, and what one must come to
understand is that both are part of the fundamental
nature of the *Tao*. If one can come to accept
suffering as easily as one accepts the pleasurable
things of life, indeed if one can come to accept death
as easily as one accepts life, then those things which
one fears will no longer be frightening. When Lao-tzu
suggests that whatever lifestyle one lives one must live
the opposite, he is not suggesting that if one is
wealthy one give away all one's riches. Rather he is
suggesting that one must be keenly aware of how
easily what one values can be lost, and that this loss
is just a further expression of the *Tao*.

It goes without saying that the social and
political philosophy of Taoism espouses complete
liberty. Any kind of institution serves only to impose
suffering on humankind, for it denies the uniqueness of
each individual. To try to make everyone the same is
to hang on to either the *yin* or the *yang* and thereby
to work directly against the fundamental nature of the
Tao: that it is ever-changing and that it is
spontaneous. Thus Chuang-tzu says:

The duck's legs are short, but if we try to lengthen them, the duck will feel pain. The crane's legs are long, but if we try to cut off a portion of them, the crane will feel grief. Therefore we are not to amputate what is by nature long, nor lengthen what is by nature short.[6]

In the end, Taoism rejects any kind of distinction, because it is an imposition on the world, and therefore false. And here Taoism points to human intellect as the culprit: it is the intellect which takes things apart and categorizes them. The world for the Taoist is a world to be fully experienced: this is another way of interpreting *wu wei*. It is to open oneself up to the world, and to allow both oneself and the world in which one lives simply "to be." Only in such harmony can one achieve peace of mind, for it is in offering resistance that we waste valuable psychic energy.

In many respects, Taoism might be seen as a naive way of looking at the world. Indeed Lao-tzu advocates that one must return to the child's way of seeing things. But to see things as a child is not to become a child. One grows up, and takes on adult responsibilities: these we cannot escape. We cannot simply "drop out." What we can do is cultivate an attitude towards the world and how we live in it. We can enjoy spontaneity in life, and can see in each passing moment the opportunity presented by the new moment. Life, in other words, is not a passing away to death; rather life is a continuous kaleidoscope of new experiences which we must live to enjoy. We must not become bogged down by worries that in the final analysis matter little anyway. What we

accomplish in life, how wealthy we become, how our
neighbours see us, matter little if the struggle takes
away the simple ability to enjoy life for what life is,
the spontaneous, ever-changing *Tao*.

CONFUCIANISM

Perhaps no other person is so associated with
ancient China as Kung Fu-tzu or, as we better know
him, Confucius (551-479 BCE).   Like Lao-tzu,
Confucius looked to find an answer to the political,
moral, and social anarchy of his times, albeit in a
very different way than his famous contemporary.
Confucius drew on even earlier sages whose works are
collectively called the *Wu Ching* or "Five Classics."
These "Five Classics" are the *Li Chi (Book of Rites)*,
a collection of rituals; *Shih Ching (Classic of Song)*, a
collection of 305 poems dating from the tenth to the
seventh centuries BCE; the *Shu Ching (Classic of
History)*, a collection of semi-historical documents and
speeches dating from the early centuries of the Chou
Dynasty; the *I Ching (Classic of Changes)*, a book of
divination based on the *yin* and the *yang*; and the
Ch'un Ch'iu (Spring and Autumn Annals), a historical
record of the state of Lu much respected by Confucius
and other later philosophers.   Confucius took much of
this traditional material and transformed it into a
coherent social, moral, and religious philosophy.
While during his life Confucius was at best a minor
government bureaucrat aspiring to high office, his
ideas have guaranteed him earthly immortality, for no
one set of ideas has ever dominated a culture as much
as have those of Confucius.   Confucius himself has
only left us a miscellaneous collection of his sayings
known as the *Analects*, but these were subsequently

fleshed out and systematized by later thinkers who were grouped together into a variety of Confucian schools.

Confucius accepted the idea of a supreme principle in the universe (*Tao*), but how he perceived this principle was radically different from what is found in Lao-tzu and Chuang-tzu. Rather than representing spontaneity and unpredictableness, the *Tao* refers to the ordered nature of the universe in which everything has a proper function. Society is the mirroring of this fundamental order in the proper ordering of human relationships. The Confucians talk of *Cheng Ming* or the "Rectification of Names," which is represented in the statement, "Let the ruler be a ruler and the subject a subject; let the father be a father and the son a son." In this statement is the suggestion that every name possesses its own definition, which designates that which makes the thing to which the name is applied. In other words, the first time the name "ruler" is mentioned it refers to the person; the second time it appears it refers to a role which entails specific responsibilities, expectations, etc. What Confucius stressed was that the ruler, the father, the son, etc. must act in real life in accordance with what these words indicate as roles in society.

Li is a term referring to these roles as they fit into the larger scheme of society. While *Li* looks outward, concerned with human deportment in society, another Confucian concept, *Jen*, looks inward at the individual who carries out the demands of *Li*. *Jen* refers to the moral and humane being, and, in the Confucian scheme of things, it is through the learning of *Li* that one inculcates *Jen*. Overriding *Li* and *Jen*, however, is that both express the harmony of the *Tao*. Thus in the *Analects* one reads:

> Among the functions of propriety the most valuable is that it establishes harmony. The excellence of the ways of ancient kings consists of this. It is the guiding principle of all things great and small. If things go amiss, and you, understanding harmony, try to achieve it without regulating it by the rules of propriety, they will still go amiss.[7]

Education is learning the rituals and various arts by which society operates, for, in being able to follow these rituals and arts, one will necessarily be a moral person.   Thus education is crucial in Confucianism, and Confucius himself is viewed as a great teacher.

In the pursuit of *Li*, one thing predominates over everything else, and stands as the fundamental building block of Confucian society. This is "filiality," which in the most general sense means respect for one's parents. Not only does it make the family the most important unit around which everything else revolves, it also indirectly establishes how government should operate. The emperor and high government officials must see themselves as parents of the people and treat them accordingly. While punishment and reward are a part of this relationship, most important is that the ruler look out for the wellbeing of the citizen in exactly the way a father and mother look out for their children; in return the people must treat government officials and the emperor in the same way they treat their parents. In the Confucian system, nothing is worse than to be guilty of non-filial activity.

THE LATER CONFUCIANS

Confucius died in 479 BCE leaving behind only a small group of followers. These disciples spread throughout the Chinese empire, although none achieved much more success than their master. At the same time, they kept alive the ideas of Confucius until the period of the Han Dynasty (206 BCE - 220 CE) when they finally found fertile ground. Among the Confucianists, two are especially important, Meng-tzu or Mencius (370 - 290 BCE), who is believed to have come from the same state as Confucius, and Hsun-tzu (298 - 238 BCE), who was a native of Chao.

Mencius saw himself as a transmitter of Confucius' teachings, and, if there are differences between Confucius and Mencius, they are entirely a matter of emphasis. While Confucius only implied that human nature was basically good, Mencius absolutely declared that humankind possesses an innate knowledge of good and an innate ability to perform good acts. If evil exists, it is because humankind does not allow for this inherent capability to develop. Thus Mencius' teachings, which are recounted in an untitled work usually called *The Book of Mencius*, stress the recovery of one's original nature. As Mencius writes, "Humanity is man's mind and righteousness is man's path. Pity the man who abandons the path and does not follow it, and who has lost his heart and does not know how to recover it."[8] To make the point that humankind is basically good, Mencius talks of how we spontaneously perform the moral act:

All men have a mind which cannot bear
(to see the sufferings) of others. . . . If today men suddenly see a child about to fall
into a well, they will without exception
experience a feeling of alarm and distress.
This will not be as a way whereby they may
seek the praise of their neighbours and
friends, nor that they are so because they
dislike the reputation (of being unvirtuous).[9]

All this begs the question, of course, as to what
Mencius means by the "good." Here he follows
Confucius in asserting an ordered nature in which
everything has place and purpose: chaos, rebellion, and
disorder comprise evil. Thus Mencius writes that
"whatever the Superior Man passes through,
transformation follows; wherever he abides, there is a
spiritualizing influence. This flows abroad and below
together with Heaven and Earth."[10]   For Mencius,
then, to adhere to order is to follow Heaven; it is to
follow the *Tao* and thereby to be at one with the true
nature of things:

He who exerts his mind to the utmost
knows his nature. He who knows his nature
knows Heaven. To preserve one's mind and to
nourish one's nature is the way to serve
Heaven. Not to allow any double-mindedness
regardless of longevity or brevity of life, but
to cultivate one's person and wait for destiny
is the way to fulfill one's destiny.[11]

Hsun-tzu, a second major interpreter of
Confucius, is considered by some scholars as a major
force in the establishment of Confucianism during the

Han Dynasty. Hsun-tzu differed, however, in a very fundamental way from his predecessors in denying the basic goodness of humankind. Men and women were evil, and education was, according to Hsun-tzu, crucial to correcting this evil:

> The nature of man is evil; his goodness is the result of his activity. Now, man's inborn nature is to seek for gain. If this tendency is followed, strife and rapacity result and deference and compliance disappear. By inborn nature one is envious and hates others. If these tendencies are followed, injury and destruction result and loyalty and faithfulness disappear. By inborn nature one possesses the desires of ear and eye and likes sound and beauty. If these tendencies are followed, lewdness and licentiousness result, and the pattern and order of propriety and righteousness disappear. Therefore to follow man's nature and his feelings will inevitably result in strife and rapacity, combine with rebellion and disorder, and end in violence. Therefore there must be a civilizing influence of teachers and laws and the guidance of propriety and righteousness, and then it will result in deference and compliance, combine with pattern and order, and end in discipline.[12]

Why humankind is evil Hsun-tzu fails to say; it is enough that such is the case and that humankind must be redirected into the path of the good. It is hardly surprising, moreover, that Hsun-tzu, given his perception of human nature, places particular emphasis

on *Li* or external action as a mechanism for achieving
Jen or internal virtue:

> Man's nature is evil. Therefore the sages of
> antiquity, knowing that man's nature is evil,
> that is it unbalanced and incorrect, and that
> it is violent, disorderly, and undisciplined,
> established the authority of rulers to govern
> the people, set forth clearly propriety and
> righteousness to transform them, instituted
> laws and governmental measures to rule them,
> and made punishment severe to restrain them,
> so that all will result in good order and be in
> accord with goodness.[13]

TAOISM AND CONFUCIANISM AS NON-ESCHATOLOGICAL RELIGIONS

When asked about death, Confucius is said to
have replied, "Not yet understanding life, how can one
understand death?" In large measure, Confucius'
answer points to a central question concerning
Confucianism and, to a lesser extent, Taoism: are
they religions at all? In the case of Confucius and
his followers, there seems to be no interest in the
superhuman realm, as the topics and concepts of their
works pertain primarily to human nature, deportment,
and social relationships. If anything, the Confucianists
espouse a this-worldly, practical humanism. In the
case of Lao-tzu and Chuang-tzu, too, there is no
concern with the supernatural or with some "other"
reality where one can be free from the suffering of
this world. Taoism, as well, is concerned with how
one can be happy in this world.

'This, then, brings one to an important concept which helps explain how and why one classifies Taoism and Confucianism as religions. The word "eschatology" comes from the Greek word "*eschaton*," which refers to the four "Last Things": death, judgment, heaven, and hell. Of particular importance in Christianity and Islam, eschatology is often seen incorrectly as a necessary ingredient of all religions. Eschatology points to how a religion is forward-looking: death, judgment, heaven, and hell are not issues of this world. For the most part, an eschatological religion is one which sees this world as a realm of suffering and evil that anticipates a better world. Obviously, then, both Taoism and Confucianism are not eschatological religions. But they still point to the idea of absoluteness in the universe, and outline how the human individual can connect with that absoluteness. This connection is not other-worldly centered, however, but is focused on how one lives in this world. Simply put, both Confucianism and Taoism are concerned with improving the quality of this life and not with working for a better life when this one is over. The radical transformation of personality that is part of experiencing the totally other is still central to these religions. What is not central is that this totally other is tied to another dimension of reality than the one in which we live.

POPULAR CHINESE RELIGION

It is perhaps incorrect to talk about popular Chinese religion, for, in so doing, one gives the impression that there is a cohesive, unified body of belief comprising an established tradition. Nothing

could be further from what is actually the case, and it
may therefore be more correct to talk about Chinese
religions. At the same time, there are a number of
basic features of popular Chinese religion, even though
these features do not themselves come together into a
unified whole. As already mentioned, these popular
practices exist quite outside the more philosophical
traditions of Taoism and Confucianism, going back
deep into Chinese history and even prehistory. It is
perhaps difficult for the skeptical westerner to take
some of these practices seriously, given that in the
west, astrology, geomancy, and fortune telling have
been reduced to the activities of the carnival side
show. But this kind of "scientifically superior"
attitude, for which there is really no justification,
must clearly be put aside if one is to appreciate how
important this popular form of religious expression is
to the Chinese people. One need only spend a few
days at any of the temples in Hong Kong to see that
this form of religious expression is vital and alive, and
has continued so for thousands of years.

Chinese Deities[14]

There is in Chinese religion no deity which
exactly corresponds with the "God" of western
monotheistic religions, although there are references to
the "Supreme Ruler in Heaven" as early as 1200 BCE.
This supreme ruler was known as "*Shang Ti*," which
means "superior *Ti*" or "superior emperor." This
Shang Ti is not so much the creator of the universe
as its governor, and there remains the concept of *Tao*
in behind everything which not even the "Supreme
Ruler in Heaven" can control. Although *Shang Ti*
was seen to hand out rewards and punishments, and

the various ruling dynasties saw themselves as receiving their legitimacy from *Shang Ti*, the "Supreme Ruler" remained a shadowy figure far removed from human concerns.

Eventually this was to change. Beginning in the early years of the common era, Buddhism moved into China bringing with it a whole array of heavenly Buddhas and *bodhisattvas*. To the Chinese, these Buddhas and bodhisattvas looked very concrete in comparison to the vagueness of *Shang Ti*; and largely in response to this, there evolved Chinese gods to which one could personally relate. It was not, moreover, a matter of there being only one deity. As Confucianism took hold, with its notions of order and hierarchy, heaven was conceptualized as a vast administrative bureaucracy governing every aspect of life. Eventually, there developed thirty-six heavens, rising upwards in levels of superiority, each with its own administrative deity. While Chinese religion today still has many gods, there are a number which stand out. These deities are largely those which achieved prominence during the Sung Dynasty (960-1279), which was especially Confucian in outlook.

First among the deities is the Jade Emperor, who is generally seen as a successor to *Shang Ti*. The Jade Emperor first appeared in the ninth century, but did not gain his place on the Celestial Throne until 1115 by decree of the Sung Emperor, Chen Tsung (998-1023). The Jade Emperor remains to this day the supreme God to whom all the other gods are accountable. Like virtually all the Chinese gods, the Jade Emperor was at one time a man, who has since been elevated to heavenly status. The Jade Emperor is said to have been the son of the ancient emperor,

Ch'ing Ti. He was so beautiful that no one could tear their eyes from him, and his intelligence and compassion were incomparable. Although he succeeded his father to the throne, he eventually gave it up for a life of meditation and reflection. When he had perfected himself, the Jade Emperor ascended to heaven, from where he descends to help all manner of people by teaching universal compassion. It goes without saying that the Buddhist echoes are obvious here. He is called the Jade Emperor because Jade is the most precious of stones, and symbolizes all that is pure and excellent.

If the Jade Emperor is the most important deity, Kuan Yin is the most popular. Her origins really lie with the Buddhist *bodhisattva*, Avalokiteśvara, who began as a male but was transformed into a female in China. Kuan Yin has her own Chinese history revealing her to be a great helper of humankind, possessed of love and compassion for all. An extension of this is Kuan Yin's role as the protector of pregnant women and a deity of fertility.

There are two other deities deserving special mention. The first is Lao-tzu, who is, not only the legendary originator of philosophical Taoism, but also seen as a deity in his own right. There is a complete history for Lao-tzu, although western scholars would label it legend, and this history reveals, as does the histories of other notable religious personalities, that Lao-tzu was not merely an ordinary person but was destined for some special task. When Lao-tzu eventually left the empire in disgust at its corruption, he is said to have sent back the *Tao Te Ching*. The second special case is Confucius, who we do know was

an actual historical personality. The worship of
Confucius started as simple ancestor worship by his
family and close followers, but gradually this
developed into a large cult. The emperor made
Confucius part of the heavenly pantheon in 1106.
Confucius today is worshipped as the God of learning,
which is consistent with his earthly role as a great
teacher.

Ancestor Worship

Nothing is more fundamental to Chinese religion
than ancestor worship, which is based on the notion
that the spirits of one's ancestors must be kept happy.
Chinese religion teaches that there are three souls or
spiritual manifestations within each individual. One of
these souls is said to rise to heaven upon death,
another is said to go into the ground with the body,
and a third is said to enter into a special ancestor
tablet provided by the family. This tablet is very
often kept in a place of honour in the family home,
but. if this is not possible, it is kept in a special
ancestor hall at a local temple along with hundreds of
similar tablets. Important is that these spirits be kept
happy. This entails a whole variety of things,
although perhaps most important is to remember one's
ancestor on the anniversary day of his or her death.
Often this remembrance takes the form of sacrificing
fruit or vegetables or foods of which the deceased was
especially fond, although one interesting form of
sacrifice is the burning of paper replicas of things
thought to be needed by the deceased. All manner of
things are burned: refrigerators, clothes, even "money
of the underworld."

While ancestor worship took on great importance because of the filial piety espoused by Confucianism, it is really an expression of the much older belief that honouring the dead placates the spirits in such a way that they remain benevolent towards the living. When a spirit is not remembered in the appropriate way, it can become a *kuei* or a ghost, and do all manner of unpleasant things. Ghosts are very much a reality in Chinese religion, and stories of evil ghosts form the staple of much Chinese literature.

Animistic Religion

Certainly the oldest form of Chinese religion is animistic in nature. The term "animism" was originally used by the nineteenth-century anthropologist William Tylor to describe that form of religious expression which conceptualizes a spiritual dimension or soul (*anima*) existing along side the material dimension. Thus a tree possesses a spirit just as much as an animal or a human being. In Chinese religion, this animism is most notably found in the idea of "spirit of place." Very often, therefore, in places of unusual natural beauty, one will find small altars on which sacrifices are left for the "spirit of place."

These natural spirits must also be kept happy, or at least kept away. The popularity of firecrackers in China stems from the belief that they frighten off evil spirits; thus on important occasions, such as a marriage, firecrackers play an important role in the proceedings. The keeping away of evil spirits also explains why temples have a dragon either on the wall of the temple or at the apex of the temple roof. The dragon is not seen as evil, but as something which wards off evil. Finally, talismans and charms play an important part in Chinese religion. One will, for example, hang a potent object over one's bed to ward off evil spirits while one is asleep.

Divination and Fortune Telling

It is difficult to determine how seriously this aspect of Chinese religion is taken by the Chinese people themselves. One hears stories, for example, of how people go from fortune teller to fortune teller until they get the answer they want. That so many people go to fortune tellers in the first place, however, suggests that the exercise has some purpose. Mediums who consult with the gods are common at Chinese temples, and outside temple walls one invariably finds phrenologists and palmists, who will for a fee foretell the future or suggest remedies for personal problems. Perhaps the most important expression of this aspect of Chinese religion is *Feng Shui* or "geomancy," which is concerned with how one finds an auspicious location for a house or office building.

CHINESE RELIGIONS AND THE RELIGIOUS EXPERIENCE

Popular Chinese religion may in some respects seem to thrive on self concern. Unlike other forms of religion, in which one praises God or the gods out of love or respect, Chinese religion puts front and center the fact that the gods and the devotee both want something. It is very much *quid pro quo.*

Fundamental to Chinese religion is the recognition that there exists a spirit world which runs parallel to the human world, and that this spirit world may work for one's betterment or may bring unhappiness and suffering. Thus humankind is simply responding to a spirit world accepted as having a vital effect on each person's life. This spirit world must therefore be accounted for in everything one does, for to do otherwise would be to ignore the fundamental nature of things.

The philosophical stream of Chinese religion might best be described as cultivating a particular mental attitude towards the world, and in this regard many might say it does not seem to be specifically "religious." Lao-tzu, Confucius, Mencius, and the many other great thinkers of China may be better classified as social and political reformers than religious teachers. Certainly there is no desire on their part to escape from the world; nowhere is there mentioned the goal of liberation or salvation. Yet they are still concerned with the ultimate transformation that is basic to religion: central in what they write is the desire to map out a path that allows us to be the best that humankind can be. With such transformation comes completeness, and thus, while these traditions might not have the fabric most usually associated with being "religious," they are as much concerned with the religious personality as any other of the world's religions.

SHINTŌ

As the indigenous religion of Japan, Shintō possesses a number of distinctive features. First, it is a religion limited to one race of people, the Japanese, and is therefore often seen, not so much as a religion, but as a way of life that makes the Japanese the distinctive race they are. Second, it is one of the oldest of the world's religions: without scriptures of any sort, it has continued uninterrupted since prehistoric times. Third, Shintō is irritatingly vague and often seems little more than disparate folk beliefs that have little real religious significance for the Japanese. Fourth, Shintō, while very much taken for granted by the Japanese, has a highly visible presence in the thousands of shrines, big and small, found all over Japan, in the tremendous popularity of the many festivals associated wtih Shintō, and in the way the Shintō priest is present on virtually all auspicious occasions.

The *Kami* Way

Since ancient times, the Japanese have accepted the existence of the *kami* or the spirits. In large part, these spirits are associated with the forces of nature: rocks, trees, and rivers are all said to possess *kami*-nature. The concept of *kami* goes beyond nature spirits, however, to include the animate world of animals and human beings. While it is accepted that all human beings possess spirits, the term "*kami*" is especially used in association with particularly noble human beings who have performed significant deeds during their lives and with the ancestral spirits of the family unit. Shintō is concerned with *kami-no-michi* or the "way of the *kami*," and to this end focuses on giving appropriate recognition and honour to the *kami*, be they ancestral *kami*, *kami* derived from Japanese history, or the celestial *kami* such as Amaterasu-Ōmikami or the Sun Goddess. All of this is suggested in the term "Shintō" itself, which is composed of two Chinese characters usually translated as the "divine way" or the "way of the gods."

Shintō possesses no developed doctrine or theology. But it does have a mythology, which, in recounting the events of the ancient age of the *kami*, outlines the origin of Japan and affirms the centrality of Japan in the events of history. These ancient tales of Shintō are vague and disjointed, comprised of an oral tradition finally committed to writing in the quasi-historical *Kojiki*, which dates from the eighth century when Chinese *kanji* found its way into Japan and the Japanese finally possessed a way of writing things down. Significant in this mythology is the appearance of the divine couple Izanagi-no-mikoto (the male principle) and Iznami-no-mikoto (the female principle). From their union came the eighty countries, the "eight great islands" of Japan, and eight-hundred thousand *kami*, of which the three most important are Amaterasu-Ōmikami (the Sun Goddess), Susano-o-no-mikoto (the *kami* of the High Plain of Heaven who rules the earth), and Tsuki-yomi-no-mikoto (the Moon Goddess). Amaterasu becomes the supreme *kami*, and it is her grandson, Ninigi-no-mikoto, who descends from heaven to rule Japan. Ninigi-no-mikoto's great grandson in turn becomes the first human ruler of Japan, the emperor Jimmu. This association between the mythological *kami* and the rulers of Japan accounts for the divine status of the Japanese emperor, which, while formally denied at the end of World War II, is indirectly expressed in the love and veneration the Japanese continue to afford their emperor to this day.

Kinds of Shintō[15]

The accepted practice among scholars is to talk of Shintō as having a number of distinct forms, albeit there is some overlap and all focus on the *kami-no-michi* central to Shinto generally.

1. Popular Shintō or Folk Shintō

This is the least tangible form of Shintō, referring as it does to the religious beliefs that go back to primitive times, and that have for the most part remained unsystematized. Folk Shinto recognizes the spiritual dimension of *kami* that lies behind virtually everything in the world. Not surprisingly, the *kami* representing fertility are among the most important, given the dependence of the people on a successful harvest. Each rice planting, for example, is preceded by the Rice Transplant Festival in which the rice shoots are offered to the *kami* for blessing. The ancient mythology of Shintō rightfully belongs in this category, although it figures, as well, in other forms of the tradition. The idea of an "other" world is present in only the vaguest way as the abode of the celestial *kami*, and there is little suggestion of life-after-death. This non-eschatological orientation of Shinto is one which pervades all its forms, affirming its concern with a happy and prosperous life in the present world.

2. Shrine Shintō

A shrine or *jinja* is considered the "house" of the *kami*, and it is to shrines that one goes to honour and pay devotion to the *kami*. Shintō shrines are the most visible sign of Shintō, ranging from the huge Meiji Jinja in Tokyo to the hundreds of small shrines that dot the Japanese landscape. The most important

Shintō shrine is the Grand Shrine of Ise, whose chief *kami* is Amaterasu-Omikami.

A distinctive feature of Shrine Shintō is the priests and other religious officials associated with the shrines. The idea of a priest in Shintō likely began with the ancient notion of the shaman, who is one who serves as a medium through whom the gods and humankind communicate. To expedite spiritual communication, the shaman performed specific rituals that would gain the gods' attention. This performance of religious rituals remains the priest's main responsibility in contemporary Shrine Shintō.

Priests today are classified into four ranks. Each major shrine has a *gūji* or "chief priest" and many have a *gon-gūji* or "assistant chief priest," as well as priests of the two lower ranks, *negi* and *gon-negi*. While the major shrines have fulltime priests, smaller shrines have either part-time priests who work in other occupations, or no priests at all. Women may become priests, although the most distinctive female contribution to Shrine Shintō is the *miko*, who are young women drawn from the local community trained to perform the ceremonial dances of the shrine.

There are a number of rituals associated with the Shintō shrine. Most important of these entail purification, which ranges from personal purification by rinsing out one's mouth and passing water over one's fingers to the purification of the entire nation by the priests. Those coming to shrines are expected to leave an offering to the *kami*, which may include money, food, or some object of particular value to the devotee. Prayers to the *kami* express thanks for past favour and request the sympathy of the *kami* in the future. Finally, there is the sacred feast, in which the devotee takes a sip of sake or rice wine served by a priest, the principle here being that one is eating with the *kami*. This particular rite is often performed by priests at events of unusual importance, such as a wedding or family anniversary.

While the operation of each shrine is independent, there does exist an Association of Shintō Shrines, which came into existence in 1946. Its purpose was to formulate a general statement of Shintō beliefs; these beliefs may be summarized as follows:

1. To be grateful for the blessings of the *kami* and the benefits of the ancestors, and to be diligent in the observance of Shintō rituals, applying oneself to them with sincerity, cheerfulness, and purity of heart.
2. To be helpful to others and in the world at large through deeds of service without thought of reward, and to seek the advancement of the world as one whose life mediates the will of the *kami*.
3. To bind oneself with others in harmonious acknowledgement of the will of the emperor, praying that the country may flourish and that other peoples too may live in peace and prosperity.[16]

3. State Shintō

Although no longer recognized, State Shintō was for a time a dominant religious force in Japan. A product of the Meiji Era (1868-1912), State Shintō was in many ways a political response to the social turmoil of the times. The Meiji Era is characterized by a

conscious attempt to modernize Japan and to do away
with a feudalism that had produced widespread
discontent in Japan. One way of doing this was to
recognize the emperor as a symbol of Japanese
greatness and thus take advantage of the emperor's
already established place as direct descendent of the
Sun Goddess. Devotion to the emperor was
demonstrated in commitment to the nation, and this
gave rise to a strident patriotism that found its most
extreme expression in World War II. Any recognition
of State Shintō ceased with the defeat of the Japanese.

4. Imperial Shintō

This form of Shintō is practised in the three
shrines within the palace grounds of the emperor. It
has no immediate significance for the ordinary person,
as the rituals are carried out, if not by the emperor
himself, then by members of the royal household.

5. Household Shintō

Household Shintō entails the worship of one's
ancestral *kami* in front of a household shrine called a
kami-dana or "kami shelf." Devotions to the *kami*
ought to take place twice a day. They entail
expressions of gratitude towards one's ancestors,
requests for help in overcoming the difficulties of life,
and offerings of food. Prior to performing household
worship, one must, as at a shrine, ritually purify
oneself by washing one's face and rinsing out one's
mouth.

The Shintō Worldview

In discussing Shintō, many reduce it to its five
categories of religious expression or see it as a rather

unsophisticated form of animism or spirit worship. To see Shintō in this fashion is to do it a great disservice, for it is equally the case that Shintō presents a psychologically coherent world view that is distinctively Japanese. Important here is how *kami* refers, not so much to specific spirits, as to a fundamental spiritual dimension that permeates and conditions the world in which we live. The fundamental feature of *kami* in this context is described by the word *nagare*, meaning "flow" and referring to the flow and harmonious continuity of life.[17]

Nagare asserts that the basic nature of reality is change. This change must not, however, be seen as decay or the flowing away of things into death; rather it is a process of continual renewal, as the passing of each moment entails the birth of a new one. Life is, in other words, a series of new challenges and new adventures. For one to live a happy and productive life, one must get in touch with this "flow of life" and turn away from a perception of reality that sees change as basically evil. In this regard, then, the spiritual thrust of Shintō is life-affirming, and it comes as no surprise that death in Shintō is the ultimate pollutant. Shintō shuns death and has nothing to say about it: it is the Buddhist priest who officiates at funerals while births and weddings are the proper domain of the Shintō priest.

To see Shintō in this philosophical way is not, however, to deny the more popular notion of *kami* as "spirit." Rather the spirits may be seen as maintaining the harmony and continuity of *nagare*. To pray to the *kami* is, then, to reach out to participate with them in this divine creativity. It is to rid ourselves of the unhappiness and frustration of life, and thereby to turn away from anything that inhibits renewal.

The Shintō shrine is very much a visible expression of the life affirming quality of *nagare*. Made of natural materials, and very often located in places of unusual natural beauty, shrines are not something imposed on the natural landscape but are a continuation of it. In exactly the same way, humankind must not intrude on the natural way of things but should be congruent with it. Nature is an expression of the potential for rejuvenation, as spring inevitably follows from winter, and the shrine, as an extension of nature, comprises a portal by which one can connect with the life-affirming quality that constitutes the nature of things. Affirming that the shrine is a portal to the sacred are the *torii* (gate) and *shimenaa* (sacred rope) that mark the division between the mundane world and the *kami*-world of the *jinja*.

That life is a thing of constant renewal is further affirmed in the Shintō emphasis on life stages. As one enters a new stage of life, one inevitably goes to the shrine. Here one does not bemoan the passing away of a previous stage of life or just-passed season of the year, but looks with enthusiasm on the new opportunities that the next life stage brings. To visit a shrine on such occasions is to affirm the constant newness of life.

The Japanese, despite centuries of cultural overlay imported into Japan, remain a people filled with enthusiasm for life, and this enthusiasm may well be traced back to the religious expression of Shintō, which is so fused with the Japanese world view that

one cannot say, as one can with other religious
traditions, that the religious domain ends here and the
secular one begins there. Virtually all the world's
religions stress that religion must be integrated with
the other dimensions of life, and indeed should
determine how these other dimensions unfold. That
one fails to heed this role of religion is humankind's
great error. Unique about Shintō is that this
integration is so naturally present that it is really
impossible to think of Shintō as an identifiable religion
and to see it instead as simply being Japanese.

Notes

[1] *Tao-te-Ching*, 25, in *A Source Book in Chinese
Philosophy*, ed. Wing-Tsit Chan (1963; rpt. Princeton:
Princeton University Press, 1969), p. 152.

[2] *Chuang-tzu*, 36, quoted in Fung Yu-an, *A
History of Chinese Philosophy*, trans. Derk Bodde;
(1937; rpt. Princeton: Princeton University Press,
1983), Vol. I, p. 180.

[3] *Tao-te-Ching*, 42, in Wing-Tsit Chan, p. 160.

[4] *Tao-te-Ching*, 34, in Ibid., p. 157.

[5] *Tao-te-Ching*, 22, in Ibid., p. 151.

[6] *Chuang-tzu*, 8, quoted in Fung-Yu-lan, p. 229.

[7] *The Analects*, 1:12, in Wing-Tsit-chan, p. 21.

[8] *Mencius*, VIA: 11, in Wing-Tsit-chan, p. 58.

[9] *Mencius*, IIa, 6, quoted in Fung-Yu-lan, p. 120.

[10] *Mencius*, VIIa, 13, quoted in Fung-Yu-lan, p.
129.

[11]*Mencius*, VIIa, 1 in Wing-Tsit Chan, p. 78.

[12]*Hsun-tzu*, 23, in Ibid., p. 128.

[13]*Hsun-tzu*, 23, in Ibid., p. 131.

[14]My discussion here relies on Jonathan Chamberlain, *Chinese Gods* (Hong Kong: Long Island Publishers, 1983).

[15]Much of this discussion comes from .Sokyo Ono, *Shintō: The Kami Way* (Tokyo: Charles E. Tuttle, 1962), pp. 1-71; and *Japanese Religion: A Survey by the Agency for Cultural Affairs* (1972; rpt. Tokyo: Kodansha International, 1981), pp. 11-45.

[16]Quoted in *Japanese Religion*, p. 33.

[17]Stuart D.B. Picken, *Shintō: Japan's Spiritual Roots* (1980: rpt. Tokyo: Kodansha International, 1981), pp. 21-24. Also see D.W. Atkinson, "Shinto, Nagare, and the Japanese Personality," *Scottish Journal of Religious Studies*, Vol. VIII, No. 1 (1987), 25-34.

Selected Readings

Chinese Religion

Blofeld, John. *Taoism: The Road to Immortality.* Boulder: Shambhala Publications, 1978.

Chai, Ch'u and Winberg Chai. *Confucianism.* New York: Baron's Educational Series, 1973.

Chan, Wing-Tsit. *The Way of Lao Tzu (Tao Te Ching).* Indianapolis: The Bobbs-Merrill Company, 1963.

Chan, Wing-Tsit. *Religious Trends in Modern China.* New York: Octagon Books, 1978.

Christie, Anthony. *Chinese Mythology.* New York: Peter Bedrick Books, 1985.

Creel, Herrlee G. *Chinese Thought from Confucius to Mao Tse-Tung.* Chicago: University of Chicago Press, 1953.

Fung, Yu-Lan. *A History of Chinese Philosophy,* 1953; rpt. Princeton: Princeton University Press, 1983, 2 vols.

Hughes, E.R. (trans). *Chinese Philosophy in Classical Times.* London: J.M. Dent and Sons, 1966.

Lin, Yutang. *The Wisdom of Confucius.* Toronto: Random House of Canada, 1938.

McCarroll, Tolbert. *The Tao: The Sacred Way.* New York: Crossroad Publishing, 1982.

Merton, Thomas. *The Way of Chuang Tzu.* Toronto: McClelland and Stewart, 1969.

Moore, Charles A. *The Chinese Mind.* Honolulu: University of Hawaii Press, 1967.

Schwartz, Benjamin I. *The World of Thought in Ancient China.* Cambridge: Harvard University Press, 1985.

Watts, Alan. *Tao: The Watercourse Way.* New York: Pantheon Books, 1975.

Japanese Religion

Ellwood, Robert S. Jr. *An Invitation to Japanese Civilization*. Belmont, California: Wadsworth, 1980.

Falk, Nancy and Rita M. Gross (eds.) *Unspoken Worlds*. San Francisco: Harper and Row, 1980.

Moore, Charles A. (ed.) *The Japanese Mind*. Honolulu: University of Hawaii Press, 1967.

Ono, Sokyo. *Shintō: The Kami Way*. Rutland, Vt.: Beacon Press, 1980.

Ross, Floyd H. *Shintō: The Way of Japan*. Boston: Beacon Press, 1980.

CHAPTER V

JUDAISM

שבת

V

JUDAISM

INTRODUCTION

Judaism, the oldest of the three great western monotheistic traditions, also typifies how the major western religions differ from the major eastern ones. While one must be careful of overbroad generalization, traditions such as Hinduism, Buddhism, and Taoism tend to see the individual as the divine. Thus in Hinduism *ātman* is *Brahman*, in Buddhism one possesses Buddha-nature, and in Taoism all that is comprises the *Tao*. Humankind's problem, as these religions define it, is that because of ignorance one is unable to experience fully this divinity. By contrast, in Judaism, as well as in Christianity and Islam, the individual is never thought of as the divine or as becoming the divine. Rather emphasis is on developing the proper relationship with God, in which God and the individual remain distinct. Thus in the case of Judaism, the Jews see themselves as the "chosen people" of God and in being so accept that there are certain responsibilities and expectations placed upon them.

HISTORICAL BACKGROUND

Judaism is the product of the ancient near east, which showed signs of civilization as early as 4500 BCE and eventually gave rise to the two great civilizations of Egypt and Mesopotamia. Civilization in Mesopotamia begins with a number of city states - Susa, Kish, Ur - and it is around these city states that the first empires were built. The northern part of Mesopotamia became Assyria and the southern part Babylonia, and Babylonia was in turn split into the upper kingdom of Akkad and the lower kingdom of Sumeria. During the third millenium BCE, the Akkadian ruler, Sargon I, conquered Sumeria to form one large Babylonian kingdom, and then about 2100 BCE Hammurabi, who is remembered as the first great law giver, overran the Assyrians to create one vast Babylonian empire.

The Assyrians were not long to remain subjugated to the Babylonians, and by about 2000 BCE there was widespread unrest in the Babylonian empire. Among those who immigrated from the empire was Terah, who, along with his family, which included the man Abraham, left the city of Ur for the land of Haran, about six hundred miles to the northeast in what is now southern Turkey. Here Terah died, and Abraham had an encounter with God.

This encounter between God and Abraham entailed a covenant which God struck with Abraham. The covenant stipulated that if Abraham would follow God's commandments, then God would make the descendents of Abraham His chosen people and place them under His protection. What is meant to be God's chosen people and what is entailed in following God's commandments is not, however, made clear, as God made only one promise and one commandment. The promise was the land of Canaan, which was later known as Palestine, and the commandment was that all males of God's chosen people must be circumcised on the eighth day after birth or upon conversion to the faith.

GOD'S CHOSEN PEOPLE

The early history of the Jewish people is recounted in the Bible, which entails all those books beginning with Genesis and ending with Malachi. Jews call this scripture *Tanakh*, a word made up of the three letters, "T," "N," and "K." The "T" stands for *"Torah"*, a word which literally means "teaching," although it is also translated, somewhat misleadingly, as "Law." In either case, Torah includes the so-called Five Books of Moses, Genesis, Exodus, Leviticus, Numbers, and Deuteronomy. The "N" refers to *"Nevi'im,"* the Hebrew word for "prophet," and includes Judges, Kings, Isaiah, Jeremiah, Ezekiel, as well as the twelve "minor" prophets. Finally, the

"K" stands for "*Ketivim*" or sacred writings and
includes Psalms, Proverbs, Job, Song of Songs, Ruth.
Lamentations, Ecclesiastes, Esther, Daniel, Ezra,
Nehemiah, and Chronicles.

Tanakh is crucial in Judaism, for it is the
historical document of a people who sees history as
belonging to God and as God's gift to His people.[1]
God is "*Yahweh*," which is often translated as "I am
what I am," although a more correct translation is "to
happen" or "to come to pass." Thus God "causes to
happen what happens," as a historical God rules over
a historical people. History here, however, should not
be construed as mere empirical detail; rather it is the
events of the past that continue to have a continuing
vitality in the life of the Jewish people. In this
context, whether something actually happened as
recounted in *Tanakh* is irrelevant; what is important is
its significance for the special relationship between
God and His chosen people. A good example in this
regard are the two stories of the creation, which
affirm that God created the universe with a purpose
and order that is to characterise the working out of
divine intention throughout all of subsequent history.
The first story is the actual creation of the universe
and all that is in it, with man coming last as the
pinnacle of God's creative efforts. The second dwells
on the creation of humankind and reveals how God
teaches Adam and Eve how to lead a righteous life
and how they, through their own disobedience, are
expelled from Paradise. This story is especially
important in Judaism, not for recounting one specific
historical event, but for the way it represents the
subsequent history of the Jewish people, which is one
of falling away from God and then finding Him again.

The key to the "religious life" or "life with God", then, is "to remember," that by remembering the past one knows how to act in the present and has some expectation for the future. While the entire Biblical text is important in this regard, a number of events loom large in this notion of "remembering": the giving of the Laws to Moses on Sinai, the Exodus from Egypt, the warnings of the prophets during the time of David and Solomon, and the captivity in Babylon. These past events of history recounted in *Tanakh* make clear just what it means to be God's chosen people now and in the future.

THE GIVING OF THE LAW

For about four hundred years, Abraham's descendents wandered as nomads in Canaan. They are often called Hebrews, the generally accepted explanation being that the word "Hebrew" originates from the word "*ever*" meaning "one who crossed over" and referring to Abraham who crossed the Jordan River.[2] Living off the land, these Hebrews were left alone by the indigenous Canaanite people, who saw as strange their belief in a God that could not be seen. As the Biblical text reveals, Abraham begat Isaac, Isaac begat Jacob, and Jacob begat twelve sons including Joseph, whose story of the many-coloured coat is well enough known not to need recounting here. During the later years of Jacob's life, a famine swept the land of Canaan, causing many hungry people to move into the fertile Nile delta in search of food. The Hebrews, we are told, were invited by the Egyptian Viceroy, Joseph. From the arrival of the Hebrews into Egypt in the 16th century BCE to their departure in the 12th century the Biblical text is silent.

Something, however, occurred to change the reception the Hebrews received in Egypt, for the next we hear of them they have been enslaved. The suggestion of some scholars is that at some time in the 16th century BCE, prior to the ingathering of the Hebrews into Egypt, an Asiatic tribe known as Hyksos conquered Egypt, founded a new dynasty, and built a capital, Avaris, near the border into Canaan. It was the Hyksos Pharoah who allowed the Hebrews into Egypt. A century and a half later, however, the Egyptians overthrew their Hyksos masters and enslaved them, as well as all the peoples the Hyksos had allowed into Egypt.

The Biblical story of Moses is another one that is well known, although it too need not be perceived as one that is literally true: what is significant is the meaning of the story and its significance in the evolving religious life of the Jewish people. Raised as an Egyptian, albeit in truth a Hebrew, Moses is said to have killed an Egyptian taskmaster who he sees beating a Hebrew slave. Fleeing Pharoah's wrath, Moses ends up in Midian, where he marries Zipporah, the daughter of the Midianite priest Jethro. It is in Midian where Moses encounters Jehovah, who identifies himself as the God of Abraham. God commands an initially reluctant Moses to lead the Hebrews to freedom in the Promised Land, and so it is that he takes them out of Egypt to wander for forty years in the desert of the Sinai peninsula.

It is on Mount Sinai that God gives to Moses His commandments, which are of two sorts. The first are the great ethical commandments which have come to be known as the Ten Commandments. The second are a series of commandments pertaining to the practical details of daily living; included here are laws pertaining to personal hygiene, diet, sacrifice, etc. The commandments are important because, not only do they ratify the original covenant with Abraham, but they also make clear the nature of God's expectations and thereby define what it means to be God's chosen people.

That there are two sorts of commandments is particularly crucial, although one must, as well, look at Exodus 19:6 to see how they pertain to the Jews as chosen people. Here God tells Moses, "And ye shall be unto me a kingdom of priests and an holy nation. These are the words which thou shalt speak unto the children of Israel." The Hebrews are described in two specific ways. As a priestly nation, Israel has a universal mission to carry God's great ethical commandments to all people. Here the Exodus has immense importance, for, in signifying freedom from physical slavery, it suggests how the role of God's chosen people, as a priestly nation, is to lead all people out from under the bondage of suffering, injustice, and persecution. All humankind is of concern to God, and Israel is especially "chosen" as an instrument by which God expresses this concern.

The commandments concerning how the Hebrews are to live is what defines them as a "holy nation." These commandments also have particular purposes. First, they are an expression of Israel's submission to divine will, and thereby underline that God's purposes take precedence over anything initiated by humankind. Second, by following these commandments Israel develops the strength to fulfil its "priestly mission." Third, these commandments mark Israel off from other people, revealing them as models for others to follow.

THE DAVIDIC EMPIRE, SOLOMON, AND THE PROPHETS

While Moses led the Hebrews out of Egypt and brought them the Laws, he died without ever stepping foot in Canaan, and it is left to Joshua, Moses' successor, to lead them into the promised land. Crossing the Jordan River, Joshua defeated the Canaanite tribes in the famous story of Jericho. This time the Israelites take possession of Canaan, unlike during the time of Abraham when they lived as strangers in the land. With the settlement of Canaan, the Israelites ceased being a nomadic people, and this had profound effects on their relationship with God. The Hebrews were now clearly tied to the land, and there was need for a different way of maintaining unity amongst a people spread out over a wide geographical area. Thus there developed the political institution called the *Shoftim* or "Judges." Each of the twelve tribes was headed by a single judge, who had ultimate authority in dispensing justice in the tribe. These judges in turn met together in the *Sanhedrin* or "Assembly." While the system of the Judges worked for about 200 years, its major weakness is obvious: it provided no strong centralized government. In time of military threat, it was accepted that God would make known a leader. It was not, however, military threat which led to the demise of the divinely-inspired Judges; rather interdependence of the tribes and increased economic interaction with other peoples of the eastern Mediterranean demanded a more efficient political organization. So there was established a monarchy with a monarch directly accountable to God.

The first monarch of Israel was Saul (c.1020 BCE), who was confirmed as king by Samuel after he had convincingly defeated the Ammonites at Jabesh-gilead. Saul's major task as king was to turn back the Philistines, a non-Semitic people who were a constant threat to the Hebrews from about 1200 BCE onwards. Saul enjoyed a number of victories over the Philistines, but was eventually defeated at Mount Gilboa and, rather than face defeat, committed suicide. It was left to Saul's successor, David, to once-and-for-all defeat the Philistines.

A soldier, king, religious leader, and poet, David was a man of many accomplishments. His long reign (c.1000 BCE) is considered epochal in the history of ancient Israel. David extended Israel by war until it controlled an area roughly five times the size of modern-day Israel. But, for Jews, David's main achievements were not as a warrior. David is remembered for making Jerusalem a holy place, for designating Jerusalem as the place for the temple, and for bringing to Jerusalem the Ark of the Covenant, which had previously preceded the Hebrews in their desert wanderings, and which was said to contain Aaron's rod, a pot of manna, and the two tablets of the Law. In many ways, it might appear that, with David and the establishment of Israel, God's promise to Abraham was fulfilled.

Such, however, was not to be the case, for what the Hebrews enjoyed they were subsequently to lose, in what can be seen as a further reenactment of humankind's initial alienation from God with the expulsion from Eden. While David expressed the intention to build a temple, God, through the prophet Nathan, denied him the right to do so, and it was left

to David's son, Solomon, to complete the task. As
king (c.973 BCE-c.933 BCE), Solomon is remembered,
not only for his wisdom, but also for the splendour of
his reign. He fortified Jerusalem, put up many royal
buildings, maintained a huge army, and built a
magnificent temple, seven years in the making.
Solomon is also remembered for bringing Israel onto
the world stage. He formed foreign alliances, himself
marrying Pharoah's daughter, pursued a lucrative sea
trade, and encouraged immigration into Israel. But
Solomon's extravagance eventually impoverished the
kingdom, although, more damning, was his lapse in
later years into idolatry and polygamy. Although
Solomon is remembered for his wisdom, he was a man
of limited sight in dealing with his own people, as he
persistently exploited them to carry out his grandiose
schemes.

Solomon's successor, Rehoboam, treated the
people no better, rebuking them when they approached
him with their grievances. As a result, ten of the
twelve tribes seceded under the leadership of Jeroboam
to form a separate kingdom of Israel in the north.
The remaining two tribes, Judah and Benjamin, were
all that remained to form the southern kingdom of
Judah. In 722 BCE Israel was overrun by the
Assyrians, its ten tribes lost, while Judah, in
submitting to Assyrian overlordship, survived; from
now on, there remained only the descendents of the
nation of Judah.

The period of David, Solomon, and the breakup
of the empire was also the time of the great prophets,
who came proclaiming divine judgment upon Israel's
rebellion and unfaithfulness, and warning of God's
wrath. The prophets address a number of specific

issues.[3]   First,   they   condemned   how   Israel   had
forgotten its purpose as a nation of God.   With the
new political order, particularly of Solomon, Israel had
forgotten   the   conditions   of   the   covenant,   as   they
entered   into   political,   economic,   and   social
relationships with other nations.   Israel had forgotten
that God's purposes were all-important, and now saw
itself as a world power which put its own interests
first.   Second, the new economic order which laid so
much stress on profit undermined the cohesiveness of
a   people   joined   together   by   the   common   purpose
determined by the covenant.   There was no longer a
Jewish   people   acting   out   God's   will;   rather   one
individual competed with another for material wealth
and prosperity.   Third, the prophets criticized how
temple practices had lost their meaning, had become
empty,   and   had   devolved   into   little   more   than   an
excuse for celebration. Without substance, the practices
of the Israelites were corrupted by those of the native
religions common in the ancient near east.   Fourth,
the   Israelites,   in   their   new   prosperity   and
preoccupation with riches, forgot that the land and
everything in it belonged to God.   A condition of the
covenant, it could easily be taken away.   Finally, the
prophets denounced power and pride in all forms, for
they allow one to forget God and one's responsibilities
to God.

The role of the prophets is clear: they came as
a reminder to the Israelites of what it means to be
God's chosen people: the prophets stress repeatedly
that to be God's people means to have responsibilities.
The prophets affirm the universal mission of the
Israelites, which they have forgotten in the face of
pride, power, and material prosperity.   They reveal,
moreover, that the role of the Israelites is not an easy

one, that temptations are many. They insist, as well, that there is no room for compromise with God, imploring the Israelites "to remember" the past and to use this as a determination for the future. Finally, it is the prophets who further reveal to the Hebrews their evolving role as God's chosen people.

Like everything comprising Jewish "history," the message of the prophets must not be considered as something applicable to one time and one place. As the prophets spoke to the ancient Israelites, they continue to speak to modern Jews. God's chosen people have a special place in history, and that special place, with all its responsibilities, the Jewish nation must never forget. The temptations, the obstacles, and the suffering associated with this role have not disappeared; indeed they are especially present in the twentieth century. Simply put, God uses His history to reveal His will, and therefore nothing must be forgotten.

THE BABYLONIAN CAPTIVITY

The security of Judah as part of the Assyrian Empire was relatively short lived, as Assyria fell to a revitalized Babylonia. Initially, at least, the Babylonians followed the pattern of the Assyrians, placing Zedechiah on the throne of Judah as a puppet-ruler. Despite the warnings of the prophet Jeremiah, Zedechiah followed bad advice in aligning himself with Egypt in revolt against Babylonia. The Babylonian emperor, Nebuchadrezzar, brutally put down the revolt, destroying Jerusalem and the temple in 586 BCE. Zedechiah, the Bible relates, was forced to witness the execution of his three sons, and was

then blinded and sent in chains to Babylon. More
than this, though, the Babylonians, desiring to prevent
a recurrence of what had happened, carried off into
Babylon all those who were neither sick nor poor.
Thus is initiated another significant period in Jewish
history, the Babylonian Captivity, when God reveals
further the special role of his people.

Although the Jews adapted to their new homes
in Babylonia, it was nonetheless a traumatic
experience for them. Foremost in their minds was
why the exile happened and how long it would last.
The immediate answer to the first question was that
the Jews had forgotten the conditions of the covenant.
But this answer only held for so long, as the Jews
began to reflect that somehow God's punishment
exceeded the crime, especially as the exile seemed to
be continuing indefinitely; it was now a matter of
children being punished for the crimes of their
parents. In response to these concerns, the prophet
Jeremiah brings a message which adds yet another
dimension to the Jews' special role:

> Thus saith the Lord of hosts, the God of
> Israel, unto all that are carried away
> captives, whom I have caused to be
> carried away from Jerusalem unto Babylon;
> Build ye houses, and dwell in them;
> and plant gardens, and eat the fruit of them;
> Take ye wives, and beget sons and daughters;
> and take wives for your sons, and give
> your daughters to husbands, that they
> may bear sons and daughters; that ye may
> be increased there, and not diminished.
> And seek the peace of the city whither I
> have caused you to be carried away

captives, and pray unto the Lord for it:
for in the peace thereof shall ye have peace.[4]

Although God tells Jeremiah that after seventy years
"I will turn away your captivity, and I will gather
you from all nations, and from all the places whither
I have driven you,"[5] there is implicit in God's
message that the enslaved Israelites are to look at
where they now live as their home. More than this,
they are to work to improve this new home, for only
in "the peace of the city . . . shall ye have peace."
Simply put, being a good citizen is a religious duty, a
condition of the covenant. What Jeremiah's message
affirms is a radical shift in Jewish thinking. Up until
now, the Jews accepted that the final realization of
God's promise under the conditions of the covenant
was tied to land; however, this seems no longer the
case. Still as partners with God, the Israelites must
work to realize the promised land where they are; it is
in so doing that they will be "gathered from all
nations." The promised land is no longer a
geographical location: rather it is a condition in which
all people will live together in joy and harmony, and
it is to this goal that the Israelites must now commit
themselves, as indeed Jews continue to commit
themselves to this very day.

THE RESTORATION, ROME, THE DIASPORA

It is not, though, as if the Jews never returned
to their homeland. Babylon eventually fell to the
Persian armies of Cyrus the Great, who by 530 BCE
controlled an empire that stretched from the Indus
River to the Mediterranean. Remembered for his
tolerance, Cyrus allowed the Jews to go home;

significantly, however, few took him up on his offer, although some Jews did eventually return to their homeland, largely due to the efforts of Nehemiah and Ezra. These Jews took with them the idea of the synagogue as the place of worship, which developed during the exile, and which continued to exist alongside the temple rebuilt in 515 BCE. Ezra the Scribe is further remembered for bringing the Law of Moses to Jerusalem, which had also taken form during the exile and was comprised of the first five books of the Bible.

The period from the fall of the Persian empire to Alexander in 333 BCE to the second destruction of the temple in 70 CE is an immensely complex one, as Judah in large part felt the effects of events in far-away places. The introduction of Hellenic ideas, with the conquest of Alexander the Great, added a new philosophical dimension to Judaism not found in the Biblical texts. Acculturation, however, only went so far. When the Seleucid Greek emperor Antiochiv IV Epiphanes adopted a policy of systematic Hellenization rather than peaceful co-existence, forbidding temple sacrifices, introducing the cult of Zeus into the temple, banning Jewish festivals, and commanding the destruction of Torah scrolls, rebellion broke out under the priest Mattathias. Mattathias' son, Judah, also known as the Maccabee or "hammer," took over from his father as leader of the rebellion. Using guerrilla tactics with the Seleucid army, Judah was singularly successful, leading his army into Jerusalem to reconsecrate the temple in 164 BCE.

While Judah and his descendents, the Hasmoneans, ruled an independent Judah for about one hundred years, eventually the Jews came once more under the domination of a world power, this time the Romans.   In 63 BCE, Pompey took control of Judah or Judea, as he called it, and the Jews became part of the world over which Julius Caesar ruled as emperor.   The history of the Jews under Roman rule is one of resistance and uprising.   It would be wrong to say that the Romans singled out the Jews for any particular kind of treatment, and Jews in fact did very well under Roman rule.   But the simple fact is that many Jews resented the Roman occupation and proved singularly uncooperative. Initially the Romans looked to rule Judea with a Jewish King, Herod, who, in doing everything he could to please the Romans, is condemned by Judaism and Christianity alike.   Herod is said to have intimidated priests, freely murdered his rivals, and, according to Matthew, ordered the execution of male infants of Bethlehem because of the prophecy that a rival would be born there.   After Herod's death, the Romans appointed his two sons to rule the Jews: Antipas was given Galilee and Archelaus was made ruler of Judea. While Antipas proved to be a good ruler, Archelaus was a despot, and eventually the Jews requested the emperor Augustus to replace him with a Roman governor.   Galilee, by contrast, prospered, and as a result became a source for increasing Roman coffers. The result here was a number of small uprisings which led to the great Jewish war later in the first century.

The two areas were eventually placed under the control of one governor.   The last of these was Florus, who provoked the Jews to such a degree that they rose in armed rebellion.   Florus had little luck in quelling it, and eventually the Roman legions under Vespasian were called in.   Actually, Vespasian did not have much more success than Florus, and it was left to his son, Titus, and the full might of Roman's crack legions to put down the Jews. In 70 CE, Jerusalem was overrun and the temple destroyed for the second time. The Jews were by no means finished, however, and over the course of the next fifty years there were two subsequent rebellions. In an attempt to break the spirit of the Jews, Hadrian made Jerusalem off limits, prohibited *Torah*, and sold into slavery those Jews who had not already escaped. It is true that in 212 Jews were made Roman citizens, but by this time they were dispersed throughout the Roman world (*diaspora*).

SECTARIANISM IN EARLY JUDAISM

It would be wrong to think of Judaism as a homogeneous religion, as there emerged within Judaism a number of groups that remained in existence until the destruction of the temple in 70 CE. These groups, which always remained a minority, are important for the effect they had on Jews in general, who belonged to no single group, and on the shape of Judaism as a religious and cultural tradition.

1. *Pharisees*

The Pharisees comprised the leading group of the Jewish establishment, even though no group in history has been as much maligned, condemned as they were for being empty legalists. It is true that the Pharisees were scrupulously dedicated to *Torah*, but this dedication was by no means a mechanical adherence to precepts of Law. Rather it demanded that service to God involve a deep internal commitment that maintained the purity of the tradition. Among the greatest of the Pharisees was Hillel (1st century BCE), who, while placing great emphasis on *Torah*, also worked to remove *Torah* from the hands of the priests and make it available to all Jews, and Rabbi ben Zakkai, who continued to work along the lines established by Hillel.

2. *Sadducees*

A much smaller group than the Pharisees was the Sadducees, who were closely associated with the temple. The importance of temple ritual to the Sadducees contrasted with the emphasis upon Law stressed by the Pharisees. The Sadducees were often criticized for cooperating too much with the Roman authorities and for minimizing the application of Law in daily life.

3. *Essenes*

Also a small group, the Essenes were rigorous ascetics who closely adhered to religious laws, and who looked forward to the coming of the *Messiah* as foretold in Isaiah, when good would finally triumph over evil. It was in preparation for the "end times" that the Essenes withdrew from society to live in cave dwellings in the desert. Scholars believe the Qumran group that produced the Dead Sea Scrolls were likely Essenes, and some have conjectured that John the Baptist also belonged to this group.

4. *Zealots*

Absolutely opposed to foreign domination, the Zealots were an extreme minority who had considerable impact in inflaming more conservative Jews to resist the Romans. They advocated violence

against the Romans, and might well be thought of as
early urban guerrillas. It is likely that the Zealots
were at Masada, the great fortress originally built by
Herod, when, in the first century, Jewish rebels chose
suicide rather than submitting to the Romans.

JEWS IN THE MIDDLE AGES

The medieval world was divided into two
religious spheres of influence. By the fourth century,
the Roman Empire was Christianized, and, as the
empire grew, so too did Christianity. The fall of the
Roman Empire in the sixth century left Christianity
well entrenched throughout Europe. In the seventh
century, Islam spread from Arabia eastward eventually
to reach India, and westward across North Africa and
into Spain. By this time, the Jews had spread out
throughout both Christian and Islamic areas. Those
that lived in Christian-dominated northern Europe
were known as *Ashkenasim*, which loosely refers to
Germany, while those who lived in Islamic-dominated
areas of the Mediterranean were called *Sephardim*.

The lot of the *Sephardim* and that of the
Ashkenasim were dramatically different. Muslim
authorities for the most part allowed Jews to practice
their religion. In the context of the sophisticated
Arab culture of the eleventh century, there developed
a highly sophisticated Jewish culture and a rich
philosophical tradition. While the *Sephardim* were
technically not equal to Muslims, they were
nonetheless free to participate fully in political,
economic, and social life, and many Jews rose to high
office. When the Christians dislodged the Moors from
Spain, the lot of the *Sephardim* degenerated, and

increasingly they were subject to persecution. In this regard, their lot became much like that of their brethren, the *Ashkenasim*, who lived in northern Europe. Jewish communities were destroyed on the pretext of destroying the enemy before going off to the Holy Land to do battle with the Arabs, and the Fourth Lateran Council of 215 decreed that Jews must wear a yellow badge and hat as a sign of reproach.

Without external support and in the face of persecution, the Jewish community turned inward to find its strength, and increasingly the rabbi or teacher became more important as an interpreter of Law and as regulator of conduct. Because of the oppression experienced in Europe, many Jews moved eastward into Poland until, by the late Middle Ages, Poland had become the center for Jewish life. While Judaism flourished in Poland for a time, history once more repeated itself. The Russian czar invaded Poland in the late seventeenth century to begin what has remained a long period of oppression for the Jews of eastern Europe and Russia.

MEDIEVAL MYSTICISM[6]

Monotheistic religions, as we have seen, tend to see God and the individual as separate, and in this regard Judaism asserts that God is the creator separate and distinct from a creation which includes humankind. But virtually all the monotheistic traditions also have a mystical tradition, which, in a way not unlike Hinduism, views salvation as a complete union or immersion with the divine; needless to say, such mystical expression is often seen as unorthodox, although it is equally true that it has enriched immeasurably the great monotheistic religions of the west. Fundamental to mysticism is the view that the divine is ultimately incomprehensible, and that in the divine all contradiction and paradox are resolved. Thus the mystic allows that God is at once personal and accessible yet hidden in being beyond thought and words.

Jewish mysticism, usually called the *Kabbalah* ("receiving"), is the product of the late Middle Ages, coming from the association of Judaism with the Arab philosophical schools, which gave Jewish thinkers the tools, as well as concepts, by which they could shed new light on their own tradition. It never, however, replaced more orthodox teachings, and, if anything, affirmed the special role of the Jews in history and made more important the relationship of God and Israel as co-workers in creation.

Among the most important of the medieval Kabbalists was Moses de Leon (1250-1305), whose principal work, *Zohar*, is a commentary on the Pentateuch, and considers the neo-Platonic notion of "emanations." According to de Leon, God, while one and perfect, is also comprised of ten *sefiroth*, which are various manifestations or emanations of the divine revealing itself. Creation was originally perfect, for, as the manifestation of the divine, it expressed the perfect interconnectedness of the one and the many. Adam's sin was that He destroyed this perfection, and therefore threatened the entire divine unity. Kabbalistic teaching, therefore, placed great emphasis on mystical contemplation as a way of correcting this damage.

Another major figure is Isaac Luria (1534-1572), who connects mystical vision to Israel's role in history.

Luria invented a new Kabbalistic mythology, which talks of a cosmic catastrophe at the heart of creation. According to Luria, God, in order to allow for the created universe, contracted into Himself. As a result, the universe cracked so that some of God's creative sparks fell into chaos. These sparks have since then yearned to return to their maker, and history is an account of the progress of this struggle. Humankind is crucial here, for it was created by God to assist Him in restoring the original perfect order. But just as God was self-alienated in His original creative act, Israel was alienated with the exile. Thus Israel's struggle to regain what it lost runs parallel with the divine initiative to regain perfect unity.

MODERN JUDAISM

During the early Middle Ages, Jews tended for security reasons to live together in a particular section of town. In time, this segregation of Jews into *ghettos* became standard practice for the Christian majority. Those Jews venturing outside the walls of the ghetto were forced to wear special badges, and penalties were imposed on those found outside the walls after dark. There were brief periods of respite for the Jews, as, for example, during the period of the French Revolution (1789), when the ghettos were opened and Jews were given full and equal rights with all Frenchmen. But these periods were few and far between.

Modern Judaism has been dominated by one event more than anything else: the Holocaust. The systematic destruction of six-million Jews in Nazi concentration camps had a profound effect on how

Jews viewed their religion. Many who survived saw in the Holocaust a challenge to their faith in a God who would allow such savagery. The notion of Israel as the "suffering servant" of God was simply not adequate explanation. At the same time, however, the common fate of all Jews at the hands of the Nazis, regardless of particular cultural background, drew the Jewish community together, and created an even greater determination to survive.

Although modern Judaism does not conform to the denominational distinctions of a religion such as Christianity, it nonetheless does possess several major wings determined by degree of adherence to *Torah* or Law. These are Reform Judaism, Orthodox Judaism, and Conservative Judaism. A fourth movement, Zionism, is a political response to contemporary circumstances rather than one specifically tied to *Torah*.

Reform Judaism, which came out of nineteenth-century Germany, was an attempt to bring Judaism into line with the contemporary world. To this end, there was a de-emphasis of the ritualistic dimensions of synagogue worship. Prayer shawls were discarded, music was introduced into synagogue worship, and prayers as well as sermons were delivered in German. Reform Judaism saw as its mission the pursuit of universal peace, and, not surprisingly, found in the "brave new world" of America an amicable home. As a consequence, the centre of Judaism moved from Europe to the United States.

In reaction to Reform Judaism, there developed Orthodox Judaism, which saw in the reform movement the destruction of authentic Judaism. Orthodox Judaism insists on rigorous adherence to *Torah*, which

it sees as defining a way of life determined by God.
This is not to say that Orthodox Judaism insists on
separation from the secular community; this has never
been the Jewish way since the days of Babylon.   At
the same time, it insists that such participation must
not compromise adherence to *Torah*.

Conservative Judaism exists at a midpoint
between Reform Judaism and Orthodox Judaism.   It
sees in Reform Judaism a dangerous willingness to
accommodate Jewish teachings to contemporary needs.
Yet it also accepts that change is necessary, as change
was obvious even during the Biblical period.
Conservative Judaism insists, however, that change
must grow from within the tradition and not be
imposed from without.

Zionism exists apart from the three major
divisions of modern Judaism, yet incorporates them as
well.   Growing anti-Semitism in the nineteenth century
convinced Theodore Herzl (1860-1904) that Jews could
only be free if they had sovereignty over their own
land.   Thus was born Zionism, which looked to
establish a modern state for Jews in the Biblical land
of Palestine.   The goal of the Zionist movement was
realized with the modern state of Israel in 1948.
Zionism continues to this day in the active support of
Israel by Jews all over the world.   To a certain
extent, Zionism has drawn Jews together, but
Judaism, like many religions today, faces the challenge
of continuing a tradition grounded on ancient practice
and ritual in a world where such practice and ritual
are less and less important.

MAJOR TEACHINGS

Torah and *Talmud*

Torah is the Hebrew word for "teaching," and generally refers to the "Five Books of Moses." It has, however, other meanings as well. *Torah* also means the Law given to Moses on Sinai, the entire Hebrew Bible, the oral law, and even all of Jewish culture and teaching. Regardless of how one applies the term, however, the crucial issue is that obedience to *Torah* is the central religious obligation of a Jew.

Perhaps the most "correct" way of talking about *Torah* is as teaching that exists in both written and oral parts. As well as the written part, God revealed to Moses laws that were not written down but were instead preserved by the prophets and eventually passed on to the rabbis. Eventually this oral law was written down by the rabbis into the Palestinian and Babylonian *Talmuds.*

Each of these *Talmuds* has two parts, the *Mishnah* and the *Gemara.* The *Mishnah* is the actual collection of laws (*halakhah*), and is divided into six orders (*sedarim*):

1. *Zeraim* ("seeds") - *halakhah* relating to agriculture
2. *Moed* ("appointed times," "holidays") - *halakhah* pertaining to festivals and feasts
3. *Nashim* ("women") - *halakhah* pertaining to marriage, divorce, vows, property rights
4. *Nezikin* ("damages") - includes civil and criminal law
5. *Kodashim* ("holy things") - *halakhah* focusing on temple rituals

6. *Toharot* ("purity") - *halakhah* pertaining to
ritual purity and impurity.

The *Gemara* is commentary on the *Mishnah* in which
interpretations are drawn and applications are made,
and it is within the context of *Gemara* that the
rabbinic tradition originated. The Hebrew word
"*rabbi*" means "master," and was originally a title
used to address scholars in ancient times. Gradually,
however, it took on the more specific meaning of one
who interprets *Torah*. In a way, then, the process
that produced the *Gemara* continues to this present
day, and this process is in turn perceived as the
continuing dialogue between God and humankind.
Rabbinic interpretation of the Law is just as much
God giving the Law today as was the case with Moses
on Sinai.

There are actually two *Talmuds*. The
Jerusalem *Talmud* was developed in Israel and
completed in the fourth century, while the Babylonian
Talmud was, as its name suggests, written in
Babylonia between the third and fifth centuries. The
Jerusalem *Talmud* is written in Aramaic with the
inclusion of Greek and other foreign terms, and the
Babylonian *Talmud* is written in Hebrew and Aramaic.
The Babylonian *Talmud*, which is three times as long
as the Jerusalem *Talmud*, is generally considered
superior.

God

In his vision at the burning bush, Moses is
given a definition of God by God: "I am He Who
brings into Being" (Exodus 3:14). As previously
mentioned, this definition is contracted into the term
"YHWH" or *Yahweh* or *Jehovah*. What this term

suggests is that God, as well as the source of all being, is also beyond all being. Consequently pious Jewish tradition forbids the pronouncement of this word, and God is usually referred to as *Adonai* or "Lord." Two additional things are forbidden Jews in talking about God: first, God must never been seen as anything but absolutely one, the suggestion being that in oneness is perfection; and second, God must never be confined to any image. As well as creating, God also regulates, and human history stands as the working out of divine will. God is also talked about as judge and father, signifying that God rules the world according to principles of justice and that this justice is tempered by love, compassion, and mercy. Put another way, God has created the universe and He cares for everything in it. This means that God cares for all humankind and not just Jews. Jews are special because they are agents of God, and serve to lead the rest of humankind to God.

Humankind[7]

Created in the image of God as God's co-worker, humankind has worth and dignity beyond any of God's other works. While history may be the working out of divine will, this in no way supercedes human freewill, and humankind is free to choose whether to work with God in making the world a better place or consciously to turn away from God in pursuing selfish interests. While the individual can sink to great depths of evil, one is not by nature irretrievable, and all persons have the opportunity to make themselves worthy by living the moral life mapped out by God's Law. Significantly, this life is lived in the world, and Judaism sees no merit in a life of asceticism. The world is God's creation and, as such, is good: to turn from it is unthinkable. Rather one must work in the world to make it the best possible place, and here redemption is very much a thing of this world. The promised land of Scripture is a symbol for a promised time of peace and harmony.

Messiah

Messiah is a word signifying "king," and outside the promise of a Messiah in Isaiah I, and references in II Kings 2, the Hebrew Bible is silent on the subject. At the same time, the idea of Messiah looms large in Jewish tradition, the outgrowth of the adversity and setbacks encountered by the Jews, particularly during the period between 200 BCE and the first century CE. The promise of Isaiah came to be taken very seriously during this period, and Jews came to expect that, as David had once been Israel's king, so would David's descendant establish a perfect society in which lion and lamb would dwell together. It was in this context that the man Jesus was seen by some Jews as the promised Messiah. Today the idea of Messiah is variously interpreted. Orthodox Jews believe in a personal Messiah, a man who will actually arrive, while Reform Jews, and especially those connected with Zionism, think in terms of a messianic age in which all humankind will be united in peace. Regardless of conception, however, Judaism, while making the matter of the Messiah a central one, places it at the end of time far removed from the here and now. In the meantime, it is the individual's responsibility to realize as much of eternity as is possible in this world, and there is therefore special emphasis in Judaism on working to make the world a better place for all.

Judaism is not an other-worldly religion, and there is an absence in the Hebrew Bible of reference to life after death or other-worldly bliss. The Exodus was deliverance from actual physical slavery, and Jewish history is one of saviours coming to lead the Jews out from material thraldom. There is no distinction in Judaism between world and spirit, and the end of Judaism is not to convert the material into the spiritual. Rather Judaism is an account of human history moving through various stages towards a reconstitution of the Garden of Eden. One does not, in other words, wish to turn away from the world to find redemption; rather one must work through the world towards redemption.

Resurrection of the Dead

Given the central Jewish teaching that the world comprises the central arena of divine intention, it is not surprising that the after life, the judgment of the dead, and the idea of resurrection do not possess the centrality found in other monotheistic religions. Even so, however, Judaism is not without eschatological teachings. During the Biblical period, there is reference to *Sheol*, which is conceived as a dark, forboding realm within the earth to which the spirits of the dead go. In the post-Biblical period, there developed the notion of the judgment of the individual in the afterlife and a consignment to heaven or hell. As Rabbi ben Zakkai writes from his sick bed:

. . . now I am being led before the King of kings, the Holy One, praised be He, who lives and endures to all eternity. If He is angry with me, His anger is eternal. If He imprisons me, His prison will hold me eternally. He

could sentence me to eternal death. And I
cannot appease Him with words nor bribe
Him with money. And furthermore, two paths
lie before me, one to the Garden of Eden,
and one to Gehinnom. . . .[8]

Concomitant with the notion of judgment, there
developed the idea of the resurrection of the dead in
this world. This resurrection takes place with the
advent of the messianic age, when all humankind will
be forgiven and be joined together in universal peace
and harmony. Saadia Gaon, writing in the ninth
century, asserts:

. . . God has transmitted to us in writing
the fact that there would be a resurrection of
the dead at the time of the Messianic
redemption, which has been borne out by
means of miraculous proofs. . . . I have
inquired and investigated and verified the
belief of the masses of the Jewish nation that
the resurrection of the dead would take place
at the time of the redemption.[9]

Worship and Ritual[10]

Nothing is more important to the Jewish
community, whether it be Orthodox or Reform, than a
sense of Jewish identity, and therefore religious
practices affirming this distinctiveness are central to
Jewish life. While the synagogue or temple, as it is
called by Reform Jews, is a center for the Jewish
community, much as is a church for Christians, many
religious observances take place in the family setting.

Central in Jewish religious practice is the Sabbath, which is comprised of the twenty-four hours from sunset Friday to sunset Saturday. As a commemoration of the Lord's day of rest, work is forbidden as the day is given entirely to refreshing body and spirit. Public worship is carried out at the synagogue or temple, although the specifics of the service vary. In Orthodox services, for example, men and women are separated and the service is in Hebrew, while the Reform service lacks elaborate ritual and emphasis is on a sermon.

The Jewish calendar has a large number of festival days divided up into three groups. The first group, called the "Days of Awe," includes *Rosh Hashana*, which celebrates the creation and is considered the Jewish New Year, and, ten days later, *Yom Kippur*, or the "Day of Atonement," on which Jews fast and pray, repenting for their transgressions and vowing to improve in the future. A second group of festivals includes *Pesah* or the "Passover," which celebrates how God "passed over" the houses of the Israelites, and the meal the Israelites ate before fleeing Egypt; *Shavuoth* or Pentacost, which commemorates the giving of the Law on Sinai, and *Sukkoth*, which celebrates the completion of the harvest. Finally, there is a group of seven "minor" festivals. The most popular of these is *Hanukkah*, which commemorates the rededication of the temple after the Maccabean Rebellion.

Other religious observances important to Jewish identity are the various dietary requirements labelled "*Kosher*" meaning "pure." These rules largely pertain to the eating of animals. For example, only animals that have split hoofs and chew their cud are acceptable for human consumption; this allows for cattle and sheep but excludes swine and horses. Meat must also be prepared in certain ways, and *Kosher* rules forbid the eating of meat and milk together. Circumcision is still a major religious observance for boys.

CONCLUSION

While drawing on history as a key to the present, Judaism is a religion that is essentially forward-looking. It is not, however, a religion which is other-worldly and whose goal is liberation from the sufferings and tribulation of earthly life. Rather Jews see themselves as playing a crucial role in the working out of divine intention in this world; the Jew is a co-worker with God in working towards the realization of a world in which all humankind can live together in harmony and peace. Judaism is a religion of pervasive hope, which finds strength in knowing that its own history is a statement by God about His creation. The sense of completeness that lies at the root of religious experience is found in Judaism in knowing that one is chosen by God for a special mission.

A striking feature of Jewish life is an immense respect for education and learning. Indeed, the rabbinic tradition is one which encourages, not only the learning of *Torah*, but of knowledge and culture in the widest possible context. One might remember all the great artists, scientists, and Nobel Prize winners that are Jewish. Such respect for learning affirms the basic recognition that the world is a divinely created arena for human endeavour. Only through knowing the world can one glorify God and work with God in bringing men and women together to appreciate its bounty.

Notes

[1]My understanding of Judaism is deeply indebted to James Muilenberg, *The Way of Israel* (New York: Harper & Row, 1961).

[2]Ben Isaacson, *Dictionary of the Jewish Religion*, ed. David Gross (n.p.: Bantam Books, 1979), p. 91.

[3]Muilenberg, pp. 74-106.

[4]Jer. 29:4-7.

[5]Jer. 29:14.

[6]I rely here on R.J. Zwi Werblowsky, "Jewish Mysticism," *The Jewish World*, ed. Eli Kedouri (New York: Harry N. Abrams, 1979), pp. 217-231.

[7]This discussion draws on Arthur Hertzberg, *Judaism* (New York: George Braziller, 1962), pp. 177-185.

[8]Johanan ben Zakar, *Berakhot* 286; quoted in Ibid., p. 208.

[9]Saadia Gaon, *Treatise*, VII, Ch. 1; quoted in Ibid., p. 213.

[10]I rely here on Isidore Fishman, *Introduction to Judaism* (London: 1958; rpt. Jewish Chronicle Publications, 1985).

Selected Readings

Agus, Jacob B. *The Evolution of Jewish Thought.* New York: Arno Press, 1973.

Breuer, Jacob (ed.) *Fundamentals of Judaism.* New York: Philipp Feldheim, 1969.

Castel, Francois. *The History of Israel and Judah in Old Testament Times.* Trans. Matthew J. O'Connell. New York: Paulist Press, 1985.

Chouraqui, Andre. *A History of Judaism.* Toronto: George M. McLeod, 1964.

Glatzer, Nahum (ed.) *Modern Jewish Thought.* New York: Schocken Books, 1977.

Goldstein, Sidney. *Jewish Americans: Three Generations in a Jewish Community.* New Jersey: Prentice-Hall, 1968.

Greenberg, Blu. *On Women and Judaism.* Philadelphia: The Jewish Publication Society of America, 1981.

Greenstein, Howard R. *Judaism: An Eternal Covenant.* Philadelphia: Fortress Press, 1983.

Kedourie, Elie (ed.) *The Jewish World.* New York: Harry N. Abrams, 1979.

Levin, Nora. *The Holocaust.* New York: Thomas Y. Crowell, 1968.

Lods, Adolphe. *The Prophets and the Rise of Judaism.* Westport, Connecticut: Greenwood Press, 1971.

Neusner, Jacob (ed.) *Understanding Jewish Theology.* New York: KTAV Publishing House, 1973.

Neusner, Jacob. *The Talmud of the Land of Israel.* Chicago: University of Chicago Press, 1982.

Neusner, Jacob. *Torah.* Philadelphia: Fortress Press, 1985.

Neusner, Jacob. *From Politics to Piety.* New York: KTAV Publishing House, 1979.

Neusner, Jacob. *Between Time and Eternity.* Belmont, California: Wadsworth, 1975.

Rose, Albert. *A People and Its Faith.* Toronto: University of Toronto Press, 1959.

Rotenstreich, Nathan. *Jewish Philosophy in Modern Times.* New York: Holt, Rinehart, and Winston, 1968.

Roth, Cecil. *A History of the Jews.* New York: Schocken Books, 1970.

Schlesinger, Benjamin. *The Jewish Family.* Toronto: University of Toronto Press, 1971.

Schneider, Susan Weidman. *Jewish and Female.* New York: Simon and Schuster, 1984.

Swidler, Leonard. *Women in Judaism.* Metuchen, New Jersey: The Scarecrow Press, 1976.

Unterman, Alan. *Jews: Their Religious Beliefs and Practices.* Boston: Routledge and Kegan Paul, 1981.

CHAPTER VI

CHRISTIANITY

VI

CHRISTIANITY

Just as Buddhism came into existence within the context of Hinduism, so did Christianity grow out of Judaism. The significant difference is that Buddhism, although adopting much of the metaphysical fabric of the Vedic tradition, was a rejection of Hinduism, while Christianity was seen by early Christians as a fulfilment of Jewish messianic hopes. It was assumed, therefore, that all members of the early Christian community were *Torah*-observing Jews. If this situation had remained, it is fairly certain that Christianity would have died out, reassimilated into Judaism. It is because Christianity gained gentile or non-Jewish converts that it split from its Jewish roots into the gentile world and evolved into the separate religion it is today.

HISTORICAL ORIGINS

Christianity begins with Jesus, who was seen by those waiting for the imminent coming of the *Messiah* as the fulfilment of Isaiah's prophecy.[1] Thus Jesus is *Christos* or the Christ, which is the Greek word for *Messiah* or "the annointed."   There is very little known about the life of Jesus, and what is known is almost exclusively limited to the Gospels of the New Testament. Because the New Testament is not simply a historical document, one must not see it as an actual account of Jesus' life, although this by no means makes it false or brings into question its value as a religious document.

Jesus, if not born in Galilee, was likely raised there. He is one of a large group of people called *Am Ha'arets* or "people of the land"; in other words, Jesus was not one of the Jewish establishment (Pharisees, etc.), but for that matter few Jews were. Nor was he associated with any particular social or political movement. The single account of Jesus' life in the New Testament focuses on his childhood up to the age of twelve when he so impressed the priests in the temple, and on the few years of his public career, which began with his baptism by John the Baptist in the River Jordan.

Tradition locates Jesus' ministery primarily in Galilee, although John mentions that Jesus was also active in Jerusalem and Samaria (Galilee, Samaria, and Judea roughly correspond to the former kingdom of Israel). Jesus was an itinerant preacher who spread his message, not by means of reasoned, intellectual discourse, but in the homely language the common people could understand. In the Gospels, he is addressed as "rabbi," but it is unlikely that he was one formally trained in *Torah*. It is more likely that "rabbi" was a title given to him as a teacher whose appeal was charismatic rather than formal.

The major drama of Jesus' life began when he went up to Jerusalem for Passover. As the most important of Jewish holidays, the Passover inevitably brought Jewish unrest for the Romans, and it was probably because of this that Pilate, the Roman Procurator, was in Jerusalem rather than in the capital of Cesaria. He was, in other words, expecting trouble, if not actually looking for it, for Pilate already had a reputation for inflaming the Jews. Although Jesus had previously performed miracles such as healing the sick and relieving those tormented by demons, and thereby suggested the presence of God within Him, it was Jesus' entrance into Jerusalem that is particularly associated with His messianic mission, echoing as it does the prophecy of Zechariah[2] concerning the coming of the King. Now a direct threat to the religious establishment, as well as an irksome political threat to the Romans, Jesus appeared before Pilate, and from his trial, it was a short and quick trip to Calvary where Jesus was crucified as a criminal.

THE TEACHINGS OF JESUS

While Jesus offered no great ethical system, and, as a Jew, assumed the great commandments of

Torah, love of God and neighbour, he clearly transformed its intent in His call, "think not that I have come to abolish the law and the prophets: I have not come to abolish them but fulfil them."[3] This transformation cannot be fully understood, however, without a second teaching, "The time is fulfilled, and the kingdom of God is at hand: repent ye, and believe the gospel."[4] In this statement, one finds a key to what Jesus means in His avowed purpose of fulfilling the Law.

Under the covenant made with Abraham, God's agreement with humankind was obey my commandments and I shall make you my chosen people and lead you to the promised land. The Abrahamic covenant was forward-looking: do something today and receive a future reward. If this statement were rephrased in more identifiable Christian terms, it would read, "repent now and you will be saved in heaven." Jesus' exhortation to repent as the "kingdom of God is at hand" turns this statement around to read, "you are saved now, therefore repent." The kingdom of God may well be seen as a future apotheosis in which one finally enters into the glorious presence of God. But it is also an inner condition that can be realized in the present, as one overcomes one's inherent state of alienation from God, sometimes called original sin, to live spiritually at one with God. Such spiritual life with God anticipates the eschatological hope of eternal life with Him.

The crucial distinction between the Abrahamic covenant and Christ's message is that salvation is no longer conditional upon one's ability to obey the Law. Rather salvation is extended through God's mercy; it is realized through divine grace. All one has to do is reach out and accept God's gift. Here, then, Law takes on additional significance: it is a means of turning one to a salvation that is already there, and serves as a way by which one accepts God's gift of salvation. What is more is that God gives humankind assistance in the act of reaching out to accept grace. He gives the potential to believe (faith), the ability to love both God and one's fellow human beings (love), and the capacity to do good works (charity). As the great medieval theologian Thomas Aquinas later puts it, humankind is freed from the fetters of sin. With awakened conscience, the individual is able to choose between good and evil, thereby consciously accepting God's gift or consciously confirming himself in the path of sin.

JESUS AS CHRIST

We have seen that in the Jewish context the notion of *Messiah* was variously interpreted. For many Jews, it was something tied to a particular person and particular events. Jesus as *Christos* is seen as the realization of this messianic expectation, even though the New Testament speaks of Jesus as *Messiah* on only two occasions (at his trial and at Paul's confession). Jesus may well have been heralded into Jerusalem as the *Messiah*, but even so, it is more by his actions than anything else that he is revealed as *Messiah*.

For the followers of Jesus, his death was a great blow, for, if deliverance was an earthly deliverance, Jesus clearly failed. Within the Christian context, however, the notion of *Messiah* was radically transformed. After Jesus' death, his followers quietly scattered, afraid for their own lives. On the third day after Jesus' death and burial, his tomb is found empty and he appears to some of his disciples; five such appearances are listed in the New Testament. This Resurrection is seen, not as the mere revival of a dead man, but as a guarantee that Jesus is of God, and that his Resurrection signifies, not just a victory over death, but a victory over sin. In other words, the death and resurrection of Jesus confirm the message he preached, that no longer are we alienated from God, but that, through God's initiative, we may enter into a renewed relationship that rids us of the anxiety and incompleteness we experience separate from God.

This message is dramatically affirmed when Christ, after appearing to his disciples at various times over a forty-day period, ascends to heaven fifty days after Passover on the Feast of the Pentecost, which traditionally commemorates the Mosaic Covenant. With Jesus' ascension to heaven on the day of the Pentecost, there is established a pattern by which the Old Testament is seen to anticipate the New and the New Testament is seen as a fulfilment of the Old. What is spoken of as an earthly deliverance in the Old Testament, then, anticipates a deliverance, not from earthly bondage, but from the bondage of sin. This deliverance is not limited to time and place, but is, in bringing eternal life with God, cosmic and apocalyptic.

THE EARLY CHURCH

The Christian Church is traditionally viewed as beginning with the Ascension, and is defined as a continuation of the community gathered around Jesus after his death. This Church of Jerusalem continued to function within Judaism, with its members attending synagogue and temple, while gathering as a "Christian" group for worship and communal activities. Central to the life of the Christian community was participation in the communion of bread and wine in which they believed existed the hidden presence of the body and blood of Christ and in which was proclaimed "the Lord's death until He comes."[5]

With Jesus' death, the early Christian community faced significant crisis. Jesus' instructions to his disciples had been to spread his message, and, as the community spread beyond the original twelve, it came to include individuals of widely divergent backgrounds. Out of this came two distinct groups, the Hebraists who were Aramaic-speaking Jews, and the Hellenists, who were Greek-speaking Jews. The original Twelve comprised the leaders of the Hebraists, while a group called the Seven made up the leaders of the Hellenists. The distinction between the two centered on *Torah* and temple and was associated with whether gentiles could be baptized into the new Church. The Hebraists insisted on strict adherence to *Torah*, including circumcision for all males who wished to be baptized. The Hellenists, while not totally giving up *Torah*, did not insist on circumcision, and supported the notion of taking the Christian message to the gentiles.

Playing a crucial role in the resolution of this first major division in the Christian community was the man Saul of Tarsus. Saul was a Pharisaic Jew, a Roman citizen fluent in both Greek and Aramaic. As

a Pharisee, he was a zealous upholder of *Torah* and a
vigorous opponent of the early Christians.   On the
road to Damascus, Saul experienced a vision in which
Christ appeared to him in the light of divine glory,
inquiring of Saul why he persecuted the early
Christians.   As a result of this experience, Saul's
convictions were reversed: he recognized Jesus as
Messiah and became himself part of the early
Christian community.

According to Acts, which comprises the earliest
"history" of the Church, Paul is important for the
major part he played in the Apostolic Council, which
was called by James, Peter, and John to settle the
controversy over carrying the Christian message to the
gentiles.   The outcome of the Council was a decisive
defeat for the *Torah*-upholding Christians, although
this does not mean there was total agreement among
the participants about what was binding in *Torah* and
what was not.   There was, however, a majority
decision to spread the Christian message throughout
the world.   Peter went off into the Jewish territories
and Paul followed a similar mission among the
"nations."   Paul is particularly heralded for his travels
in the Mediterranean world, which are so well
documented in his Letters.   Even though a Hellenist,
Paul would still from time to time visit the
synagogue, and it was on one such occasion that he
was arrested in Jerusalem for breaking *Torah*.   After
some months of imprisonment, Paul exercised his right
as a Roman citizen to have his case heard by the
Emperor.   This, however, did him no good, as he
appeared before Nero, himself no lover of Christians,
and was subsequently beheaded.

It should be pointed out that the Church in Jerusalem did not immediately die out. Under James the Just, it remained zealously *Torah* upholding. In the face of the rabbinic revival of the second century, however, those who wanted to be both Jews and Christians found themselves in a difficult position, and the Jerusalem Church eventually disappeared.

TEACHINGS OF THE EARLY CHURCH

The teachings of the Early Church are for the most part encapsulated in short statements of doctrine called *kerygma* ("proclamation"), which are the basis of the preaching of Jesus' disciples and which are incorporated into several of the Letters of Paul, as well as the Acts of the Apostles. The basic formulation of the *kerygma* is as follows:

1. The prophecies of the Hebrew Bible are fulfilled; the *Messiah* has come.
2. He was born of the seed of David.
3. He died, in accordance with the Scriptures.
4. He was buried.
5. God raised him from the dead.
6. He was raised to the right hand of God.
7. He will return as Judge and Saviour of men.

This is the *kerygma* as it exists in its most fundamental form, but, like just about everything else, it was inevitably influenced by the rich philosophical tradition of Greece. Famous here is the prologue to the Gospel of John, which is written in strikingly different language associating Christ with the divine creative power:

In the beginning was the Word, and the Word
was with God, and the Word was God.
The same was in the beginning with God.
All things were made by him; and without
him was not any thing made that was made.
In him was life, and the life was the light of
men. And the light shineth in darkness,
and the darkness comprehended it not.[6]

THE WRITING OF THE GOSPELS

The Gospels are a further sign of the
establishment of the Church. The word "Gospel"
comes from the Greek "*evangelion*" or "good news,"
and refers to those books of the New Testament that
recount the life, death, and resurrection of Jesus as
the fulfilment of the Jewish expectation and as a
signal that sin and death are vanquished. Three
things were crucial to the development of the Gospels.
Christ had promised to return at the end of time.
The world had not, however, passed away and Christ,
while expected, had not yet arrived. This, coupled
with how those who had witnessed firsthand Christ's
ministery were dying out, demanded that the
foundation of the Church continue in some other way.
The memory of Christ and his message was thus
committed to writing. Finally, the spreading of the
Church throughout the Mediterranean world demanded
a secure base grounded in the actualities of Jesus'
ministery.

As for the Gospels themselves, Matthew, Mark,
and Luke are very similar and are called the
"Synoptic Gospels," while John, influenced by Greek
thought, stands by itself. A major concern among

Biblical scholars is how the similarities among Matthew, Mark and Luke came about. While there are a number of theories, the most accepted is referred to as the "Two Document Theory." Important is how Matthew and Luke each contain material they share with Mark. The "Two Document Theory" concludes from these details that Mark is the oldest of the Gospels, from which Matthew and Luke borrow. That Matthew and Luke also contain common material not found in Mark further suggests that they draw from a second common source which is unknown and to which is given the title "Q" (from the German "quelle" meaning "source"). The "Two Document Theory" by no means exhausts the possibilities, as there have been many refinements of the theory. One such refinement suggests two additional documents, one called "M," for material found only in Matthew, and one called "L" for material found only in Luke.

The origins of John pose complex questions, as the fourth Gospel is a combination of many themes, some derivative and some original. Overriding everything else in John is the central message that Jesus of Nazareth is an embodiment in time and space of the universal reality; or, as it is called in John, the "word" or the creative principle of the universe become flesh. Such a concept is quite foreign to the "Hebraic" nature of the Synoptics. Scholars conjecture that there were a number of influences shaping John, one of the most obvious being the Greek world view pervasive at the time.

Exact dates for the writing of the Gospels are impossible to determine. Mark, as the earliest, is generally placed about 65 CE, although some scholars place it as late as 80 CE. Matthew also has both a late and early date: some suggest between 90 and 100 CE, others between 80 and 90 CE. Luke is usually dated between 80 and 85 CE. Just as the sources of John pose great difficulties for scholars, so too does a determination of its date. Fragments of John exist on Egyptian papyrus dated about 150 CE and the whole Gospel exists on a papyrus of 200 CE. It has been argued that, for the Gospel to have reached Egypt by this time, it must have been written between 90 and 100 CE.

CHALLENGES TO THE EARLY CHURCH

By the end of the first century, the Christian Church had spread throughout the Roman Empire. While Christianity was certainly flourishing, it did so in the face of considerable opposition, both direct and indirect. The most obvious threat to the early Church came from its persecution as a religious minority. Things were bleak for the early Christians during the reigns of Caligula (37-41), Nero (54-68), and Domitian (81-96), and the Christians were systematically persecuted under Decius (249-251). Reasons for persecution were many and varied. Most obvious is that early Christians, in not participating in state religion, posed a threat to the stability of the empire. As well, much persecution was localized, usually resulting from a distorted view of the Christian community. The early Christians were, for example, accused of cannibalism, child sacrifice, sexual perversity, etc.

Other threats to the early Church were indirect; here two should be noted: Gnosticism and Greek philosophy. Gnosticism (from Greek *gnosis* meaning "knowledge") is thought by some scholars to have grown out of Christianity in the second century. Most certainly it shares much Christian teaching, although it is also different from its Christian roots, and was soon criticized by Christian leaders. Gnosticism teaches that the world is fundamentally evil, and became so by divine mistake. Some human beings possess elements of the divine, but are unfortunately trapped in the world. Through the possession of a secret knowledge revealed by the Redeemer in human form, these persons can rejoin the Divine again. Especially disturbing to the Christian community about Gnosticism was that it could easily be mistaken for Christianity. Therefore Christianity was forced to define its own teaching by determining what comprised the New Testament, which was established sometime before 400 CE. Here the writings of Paul are of particular importance for how they focus on what Jesus means for the present life of the Church.

There is no question that Greek philosophy intellectually enriched early Christianity. It did not, however, exercise only a positive influence, and, in its own way, it was as much a serious threat to the early Church. A result of the coming together of Christian faith and Greek philosophy was the theological controversies of the fourth and fifth centuries. Perhaps the most bitter of the theological debates centered on the concept of the Trinity. The religious experience of the early Christian Church had encountered God in three fundamental modes: first, it had experienced the God of the Old Testament, who, in His covenant with Abraham, served humankind as a father cares for his children; second, it had experienced the Word made flesh in Christ to mediate between the Father and His children; third, it had experienced the continued spiritual presence of God in the Church. Thus there was a transcendent, mediational, and imminent mode of God, identified as the Trinity of the Father, Son, and Holy Ghost. The fact of the Trinity was not, however, the issue; rather the problem lay in the nature of the relationship among the three modes. The general view of the Trinity was "three persons in one Godhead." Subsumed to this general view, however, were all manner of possibilities. There were those, for example, who claimed the Father descended into the virgin, was Himself born and suffered; in other words, the Father was Jesus Christ. Others saw Father, Son, and Holy Spirit as aspects of one substance. Still others believed Christ's humanity was not genuine but an appearance. One of the most important of these positions was articulated by Arius, who asserted that the Son had a beginning while God was without beginning.

It goes without saying that such differing opinions were a threat to the unity of the Church. Beyond this, however, Christianity had by the fourth century become a powerful cohesive force in the Roman Empire; anything which led to the destabilization of Christianity in turn led to the destabilization of the empire. So in 325 the emperor Constantine called a council of about three hundred bishops drawn from all parts of the empire to resolve the doctrinal conflict plaguing the Church. The Council was brought together in Nicea and the result was the Nicene Creed, which was further fleshed out in a second council held at Constantinople in 381. The Nicene Creed is a formulation of the position held by Athanasius (295-373), the Bishop of Alexandria, and remains to this day one of the most fundamental documents of the Christian Church. It reads:

We believe in one God the Father almighty, maker of heaven and earth, and of all things visible and invisible; and in one Lord Jesus Christ, the only-begotten Son of God, begotten of the Father before all ages. God from God; Light from Light; true God from true God, begotten, not made, who is of one substance with the Father, and through whom all things were made; who for us men, and for our salvation, came down from heaven, and was incarnate by the Holy spirit of the Virgin Mary, and was made man; and was crucified also for us under Pontius Pilate; he suffered and was buried; and the third day he rose again in accordance with the scriptures, and ascended into heaven, and is seated at the right hand of the Father; and he shall come again, with glory, to judge both the living and the dead; and his kingdom shall have no end; and we believe in the Holy Spirit, the Lord, the Life-giver, who proceeds from the Father, who with the Father and the Son together is worshipped and glorified, who spoke through the prophets; and we believe in one Catholic and Apostolic Church; we acknowledge one baptism for the remission of sins; and we look for the resurrection of the dead, and the life of the Age to Come. Amen.[7]

This document did not absolutely end controversy, and two more ecumenical councils were called, one at

Ephesus in 431 and another at Chalcedon in 449, both of which reaffirmed the Nicene Creed. But even so it remains perhaps the most important Christian document outside the Scriptures.

THE MEDIEVAL CHURCH

It is not uncommon to talk of the "Dark Ages," which lasted for several centuries after the collapse of the Roman Empire. While the word "dark" may aptly describe the cultural and political circumstances of the time, Christianity by no means died out, and was, in large measure, responsible for maintaining a sense of cultural continuity. Moreover, it was only the western part of the empire which collapsed to the German invaders, while the east remained intact, at least until the seventh century when the Arabs swept eastward into India and westward into North Africa. This stability of the eastern Greek-speaking part of the empire is important because it allowed for the development of a very different kind of Church than that of the western Latin-dominated part of the empire. In the west, Rome was sacked by the Goths in 410, and out of this the Bishop of Rome took on increasing importance as both a spiritual and political leader, and the Church of Rome became the dominant and eventually only Church in the west.

Much has been written to criticize the medieval Church of Rome, and, while it is true that the Church was increasingly consumed by secular interests, it is also the case that the medieval Church produced some of Catholicism's most fundamental institutions and teachings. This is particularly so with respect to ecclesiology or Church structure, liturgy and worship, canon law, and theology. The Church contributed much, as well, to the remarkable artistic and cultural developments of the late Middle Ages and Renaissance, which remain to this day monuments to human accomplishment and to the glory of God.

One cannot pass over the medieval Church without particular mention being made of St. Thomas Aquinas (1225-1274), whose *Summa Theologica* stands as one of the most remarkable theological treatises ever written and one of the most important philosophical documents of the Christian Church. Aquinas is also important for how in a work like the *Summa* he expresses what the Church was thinking during the Middle Ages. Fundamentally an optimist, Aquinas, while accepting the doctrine of original sin, saw how through grace humankind became capable of great and wonderful things in the world. Aquinas dwelled at length on the relationship between reason and faith, and, although he accepted that reason can take one only so far, and that there is a definite point at which reason breaks down in the face of faith, he saw reason as an important way in which one comes to know God. Reason, as others after Aquinas also argued, should be used to understand the world in which we live, for in understanding that world we come to a greater appreciation of God's creative powers and thereby glorify God.

RIFTS IN THE MEDIEVAL CHURCH

A dominant feature of the several centuries following the collapse of Rome was the acceptance of a harmonious Christian world order; thus the word "catholic," which means "universal." Membership in society demanded that one be part of the Christian community; not to be of the Church was to be an outcaste in society. The Jews, for example, were not baptized and therefore not part of the community. The central question in this society was that if society was a body, what or who made up its head? Everyone agreed that it was Christ, and thus it was generally accepted that Christ directed both the secular and spiritual arms of society. Christ was not, however, an earthly ruler, and so it was generally accepted that Christ delegated His responsibilities to earthly representatives.

But this only begged the question, for, if there were two arms of society, were there two heads of society? The popes very early on determined themselves Vicars of St. Peter and soon raised this status to Vicars of Christ. The kings and emperors, however, also claimed divine authority. While the distinction seems clear enough, that the king ruled society and the pope ruled the Church, each arm insisted on dominating the other. The king saw the Church as part of society and asserted the secular arm over the spiritual arm of the pope. By contrast, the Church insisted that the state without the Church was nothing: just as the spirit gave life to the body, the Church determined the motions of the state. The state, in carrying out its temporal function, was therefore exercising an authority delegated to it by the Church.

The strength of the secular arm is most obvious during the reign of Charlemagne in the early ninth century, and this strength remained until well into the eleventh century. Charlemagne, not only sat in judgment on Pope Leo II (795-816), but forced the pope to confirm him as Holy Roman Emperor. Charlemagne saw the pope as simply the chief of his bishops. This situation was challenged by Pope Gregory VII (1073-1085), who, during the reign of the German emperor, Henry IV (1056-1086), clearly aspired to be a secular ruler. The confrontation between the two culminated in Gregory's excommunication of Henry, and Henry's election of a new pope. This led, in turn, to a period of open warfare, which resulted in Henry's eventual submission to the pope, now possessing a new role as secular ruler. Perhaps the most powerful of these popes, who were as much secular rulers as religious leaders, was Innocent III (1198-1216), who claimed that the world is *ecclesia* or the Church over which the pope, as Vicar-General of Christ, had complete authority.

While the Church during Innocent's reign exercised its greatest authority over monarch and state, there was never any final resolution to the conflict between monarch and pope. Very simply, the pope was constantly working to maintain the balance of power in his favour, and as more and more of the Church's energies went in this direction, the perception grew that the Church, not only threatened the secular arm, but also, in its preoccupation with worldly matters, was neglecting its spiritual responsibilities. By the twelfth century, there was a pervasive anti-papal sentiment, inspired by the perceived gulf between the Church's claim to spiritual power and the apparent spiritual poverty of so many of its actions. Most vehement of the Church's critics was the German emperor Frederick II (1212-1250), who deplored the growth of papal power and argued for reform of the Church. That Frederick's claims about the Church hit the mark is perhaps no better revealed than in 1246 when Pope Innocent IV took part in an attempt to murder Frederick. While Frederick escaped, his descendents were not so lucky. Frederick's son Manfred was killed in battle by the papal forces of Clement in 1206, and Clement subsequently began a systematic purge of Manfred's children. What these papal actions confirmed to many was that the Church was spiritually bankrupt; not surprisingly, the concerns expressed by Frederick grew. Moreover, these concerns began to take specific and concrete form, and thus was set in motion the forces that led eventually to the Reformation.

ANTICIPATION OF REFORM

The Reformation as a religious movement did not just simply start, and the seeds of the Reformation existed long before the sixteenth century. What people criticized the Church for in the thirteenth century remained, in fact, those things about which they complained throughout the Reformation. Here one can identify a number of specific criticisms often repeated in the literature of the time.

Significant in the medieval Church was a highly controlled legal system, which affected virtually every aspect of an individual's life. It was argued that, while the New Testament provided general moral guidance, it could not possibly deal with every contingency of daily life. Therefore it was necessary that there be some kind of application of the general principles provided by the New Testament. This method of application was known as casuistry. The motives here seem quite justifiable; others, however, saw things differently. While the Church might argue that it was a divine institution controlling a divine society, it was perceived by its critics as a legal institution controlling a legal society. Law became the all-consuming thing. Increasingly, critics pointed to how this canon law had lost sight of the original teachings of the New Testament, and how it had become a mechanism for perpetuating the Church's authority.

Critics further asserted that the Church's preoccupation with legalism was at the expense of fulfilling its pastoral responsibilities. Preoccupation with the legal niceties of religious jurisprudence became the chief occupation of those at the top of the Church; they were the policy makers, and had no time for the actual spiritual needs of the common people. The result of this orientation was that very minor Church officials, often illiterate and ignorant of Church teachings, became for the common people the Church's official arm. While there were many conscientious priests who did their job well, critics insisted that the Church had, for the most part, completely lost sight of pastoral responsibility in its preoccupation with Law, which had become so complex that few could understand it anyway.

Another concern was the general "worldliness" of the Church, which seemed too much preoccupied with amassing material riches. Here a number of things drew the ire of the critics. The Middle Ages is remembered as a period when the great cathedrals were built, ostensibly, at least, to the glory of God. As the cathedrals were built by professional workmen, the Church needed enormous sums of money, which it largely raised in two ways: through relics and through chantry chapels. As a physical object directly associated with a saint, a relic was considered to bring spiritual rejuvenation to anyone who touched it. In order to have relics, then, a church or cathedral had first to have a saint. This the pope would supply for a price, and, from charging admission to touch the relics, the individual cathedral got back its original investment, and, it was hoped, made a profit. To critics, the idea of relics suggested that salvation could be bought in exactly the same way anything else could be bought. Not only did such a transaction cheapen religious life, but it flew full in the face of the fundamental Christian notion that salvation is given. The building of chantry chapels was another money-making scheme. These chapels were financed from the wills of wealthy people for the saying of daily masses for their souls, and, from the fourteenth century onwards, they came to clutter cathedral buildings. Once again, critics saw this as a crass pandering to the wealthy, who could afford to buy salvation.

Particularly onerous to Church critics was the idea of the indulgence, which, as we shortly shall see, was a major issue in Luther's difficulties with Rome. An indulgence is a sum of money paid to the Church for the Church's intercession in the forgiveness of sins, and it was seen by its critics as yet another way the Church was raising money to support secular activities. The history of the indulgence is an interesting one, beginning as it does with the notion that confession for sin was central in the devotional life of the individual Christian. That one confess one's sins to God, however, was in time not considered sufficient: one must also make up for one's sins. Thus it came to be that repentance was only considered genuine if one was committed to penance: the more seriously the individual pursued penance, the more sincere was the repentance. Such a relationship led to extremes, and penance was often harsh and cruel. As well, it was possible that one might die before penance was complete, and thus there developed the notion of purgatory where penance could continue.

In the seventh century, one hears for the first time of what might be called "vicarial penance," in which another person performs one's penance. While such vicarial penance was initially voluntary, it proved impossible to keep money out, and more and more there are cases of one individual paying another to do his penance for him. Eventually this middle man was eliminated altogether. One paid the Church directly and the Church then interceded on one's behalf. Such financial arrangements were called indulgences, which were perceived by the Church's critics as an another expression of the mistaken perception that one can buy salvation.

LUTHER AND THE REFORMATION

There is no one date on which the Reformation began, and in this regard it is not inaccurate to see the Reformation as a focusing of the criticism of the Church that had been growing for several hundred years. It is generally agreed, though, that Martin Luther (1483-1546) was instrumental in orientating this focus in such a way that it led eventually to a break from the Church of Rome. Luther, an Augustinian friar, had seriously questioned things about the Church since he initially took orders, although it was the so-called Indulgence Controversy which was a catalyst for

Luther's career as a reformer. Pope Julius II (1503-13), wishing to rebuild the basilica of St. Peter's, inaugurated the Jubilee Indulgence, which was subsequently carried on by his successor Leo X (1513-21). In Germany, however, the young Albert of Hohenzollern would only allow the indulgence if he received half the proceeds, with which he wished to pay off his debts to the banking house, the Fuggers. Albert was himself a bishop of the Church, and it is an interesting reflection on the Church that Albert's debt of 34,000 ducats was what he paid to the Church to be allowed to hold three episcopal sees as a minor.

Luther was shocked by the secular tone of the indulgence, which actually had three parts. First, it gave complete remission of sin, as well as of punishment of sin in purgatory, after absolution by a confessor. Second, it assured the purchasers and their departed relatives eternal participation in the merits of the saints. Finally, it obtained for the dead in purgatory complete remission of all sins without confession or contrition. What disturbed Luther was not only the notion of buying salvation, but how the Pope was functioning as God.

The matter of indulgences came to a head in the controversy between Luther and Johannes Tetzel (d.1519), a friar of the Dominican monastery at Leipzig, who was chosen as the chief commissary of the sales. Luther's position on the Jubilee Indulgence was clearly stated in the Ninety-Five theses, which he offered for academic discussion and debate, and which are said to have been nailed to the Church door at Wittenberg. The story of Luther from this point on is a complicated one, tied as it is to both religious

and political events. Eventually he was
excommunicated by the Pope, and with this
excommunication a new chapter in the Christian
Church was underway.

THE SPREAD OF THE REFORMED CHURCH

While Luther might be recognized as the first
and perhaps most important reformer, the Reformation
owes as much to other individuals as well. Among
these reformers are Huldreich Zwingli (1484-1531), who
was instrumental in the spread of the Reformation in
Switzerland, and Philip Melancthon (d. 1560), who, as
a humanist, introduced a modifying influence into the
ideas of Luther. Most important of the second
generation reformers, however, was John Calvin
(1509-1564), who is largely responsible for
systematizing Reform theology in his great work, *The
Institutes of the Christian Religion*, first published in
1536. Calvin, who led the Reformed Church in
Geneva for much of his life, stands as the most
important of sixteenth-century Protestant theologians,
and it is to his writings that one must go to get a
thorough sense of Reform thinking.

The Reformation did not stop with Germany
and Switzerland, and eventually all of northern Europe
was Protestant. An interesting chapter here is the
development of Protestantism in England, largely
because England played such a crucial role in
European politics of the sixteenth and seventeenth
centuries, and also because the Reformation in
England exemplifies the pervasive marriage of religion
and politics in the Christian Church generally. It was
Henry VIII (1491-1547), who introduced Protestantism

into England, albeit it was a Protestantism which differed little from Catholicism, except that Henry rejected the Pope as Head of the Church. As is well known, Henry's break with the Church was tied to his desire for an annulment from his wife Catherine (1485-1536) so that he could marry Anne Boleyn (1507-1536). It was this, moreover, that produced a situation whereby Henry could use Protestantism as a means of distancing himself from and eventually breaking with the Pope, and thereby asserting England's political independence from Rome.

Reformation under Henry proceeded cautiously, although by his death it was firmly established in England under the capable leadership of Thomas Cranmer (1489-1556), the Archbishop of Canterbury. When Edward VI (1537-1553), the son of Henry's third wife, came to the throne, he was a sickly child of nine, and the kingdom was ruled for him, first by the Duke of Somerset and then by the Duke of Northumberland. Both these men supported reform along Protestant lines, and great strides were made. Most notable of these was the composition of the *Book of Common Prayer*, which, while having gone through a number of revisions since its introduction in 1549, remains a basic document of the Church of England and Anglicanism and Episcopalianism worldwide. It is true that Protestant reform was interrupted in England during the reign of Mary Tudor (1553-1558), who, as a Catholic, tried to turn things around. But her reign was relatively short-lived, and during the reign of her sister Elizabeth I (1558-1603), perhaps England's greatest ever monarch, Protestantism became firmly established and has remained so to the present day.

A significant feature of the Elizabethan Church was its comprehensiveness, as Elizabeth herself desired a church that could accommodate the needs and wishes of all Protestants, and indeed all Christians. Behind this wish was the political necessity of uniting England against her European foes, notably France and Spain. The *via media* or middle way avoiding extremes has remained a dominant feature of Anglicanism to this day, as one finds a remarkable variety of religious expression within the Church of England, as well as within those churches in North America recognizing the Archbishop of Canterbury as spiritual head.

Another case worth mentioning is that of Scotland, largely because in no single country did the Reformation take such a grip on the Church. Scotland's Reformation began with John Knox (1515-1572), a Catholic priest born of peasant parents, who in 1546 began openly to attack the Catholic Church. He was driven into exile by the then Catholic court, but he returned to Scotland in 1559, when he became the leader of the Protestants in Scotland. Knox was a committed Calvinist, and this had a profound effect in shaping the Scottish Church, which remains Calvinist today. As well, he espoused a form of democratic church government modelled on the apostolic church. This form of church government, which is called presbyterianism and which he articulated in his *Book of Discipline* (1560), replaced episcopalianism, which entails a hierarchical series of church officials from archbishop downwards, and which distinguishes the Church of England from the Church of Scotland.

THE REFORMATION--ITS THEOLOGICAL UNDERPINNINGS

While, like any great religious movement, the Reformation is comprised of numerous strands, there is a fundamental theological viewpoint which all reformers accepted. Theology begins in religious experience, and Reformed theology begins with the religious experience of Luther. The Augustinian monastery at Erfurt, into which Luther was ordained priest, was strictly orthodox in its theology. There was emphasis on God's sovereign will, and human freedom of will, that, while God was the determining force in creation, the individual was given freewill to accept or reject God's offer of grace. The priesthood dispensed grace through the sacraments (baptism, confirmation, penance, eucharist, extreme unction, marriage, ordination), and these sacraments miraculously sanctified the individual.

It was after Luther's first celebration of mass that he began to have serious doubts concerning his own righteousness. No matter how meticulously he observed the demands of his order, he could not find a merciful God and nowhere could he find absolute certainty of his personal salvation. Luther, in examining his life, found that he was not leading the perfect life of love of God, and, despite his use of penance, he was constantly aware of his imperfections. Simply put, he could not be certain that God, as stern judge, would find enough merits in him to save him from eternal damnation. Underpinning this anxiety was the unsettling notion that one actually earns one's salvation through works, which runs counter to the entire notion of Grace. Given these concerns, it is understandable why Luther reacted so sharply to such things as indulgences, for, to him, this seemed a simple-minded way to prop up a theology which was fundamentally flawed.

Luther's theology may well have seemed startling in the context of Catholic orthodoxy of the sixteenth century, but Luther himself argued quite the contrary. Luther traces his ideas back to St. Augustine in the fourth century, and ultimately to St. Paul, on whom Augustine based much of his theology. As we have seen, the orthodox view was that God extended Grace, and humankind, freed from the fetters of sin, consciously accepted it. Luther insisted that the individual has nothing to do with his own salvation, and that the initiative is totally God's. Here, he looks, as did Augustine, to Romans, where Paul writes, "For those whom he foreknew he also predestined to be conformed to the image of his Son . . . and those whom he predestined he also called; and those whom he called he also justified; and those whom he justified he also glorified."[8] From this, Luther concludes that Grace is inevitable--there is no conscious response from the individual. The Holy Spirit moves within the individual, and thereby the individual is made just in God's eyes. As a result of this justification, he is capable of being sanctified or doing good deeds.

In that the individual takes no role in his own salvation, there is a dramatic shift in the orientation of Christian life, as Luther saw good deeds, not as a means to salvation, but as a way of being assured of salvation. Luther's main concern was that he would never be able to live a sufficiently righteous life to be saved. This is now not necessary. God does everything, so it is a matter of looking within oneself to determine the presence of those signs that indicate one has been called by God. One still pursues the righteous life, but now no longer because it earns salvation but because it demonstrates salvation has been given.

There is a further implication of Luther's theology, which, while present in what he himself wrote, was not really made clear until John Calvin's *Institutes of the Christian Religion.* If God initiates everything, the fact that there are so many who still obviously live in sin suggests that God does not extend Grace to everyone. Thus Calvin articulated the notion of predestination and election, which Paul first mentions, but which Calvin, with his theologian's mind, worked out to its logical conclusion. God determines with Himself who will be saved and who will not. Those who will be saved He justifies through faith, so that faith becomes the most crucial sign of election. The remainder, the reprobate, remain in sin, and are condemned to eternal perdition.

Most certainly there is a harshness in predestination, and, needless to say, the doctrine did not go unchallenged. At the same time, one must appreciate that Calvin assumes, as do all Protestant writers and preachers, that he is speaking to the elect, and he assumes that all who hear are called. As well, there is the further implication that the ability to hear what the preacher is saying and adhere to what he preaches is only possible if one is already possessed of the Holy Spirit. Finally, and of greatest importance, is the recognition that God is so far beyond humankind that one should not dare to presume that one can cooperate with God in the working out of individual salvation. The thrust of predestination, then, is not to fill one with despair, but, in stressing the great distance between God and humankind, to affirm the glory of God.

Such a theology has implications for virtually every aspect of the Church. Because God works directly in the individual, the intermediary of the priest is no longer necessary, and the sacraments seen as so important in the Catholic Church lose their significance. Generally speaking, the only sacraments retained by the Protestant Churches are baptism and the eucharist, and these are largely relegated to being commemorative ceremonies rather than ones that initiate spiritual transformation. Because God speaks directly to the individual, and because God's statement to humankind is the Bible, the Reformation also provided impetus for the translation of the Bible into languages people could understand--no longer was there only a Latin text. As well, the Reformation produced an aversion to ecclesiastical authority and replaced it with a Church in which each member had a voice.

THE EASTERN CHURCH (ORTHODOX CHURCHES)

While Protestantism and Catholicism represent two great groups within Christianity, there is yet a third group, generally known as the Eastern Orthodox Church or simply as the Eastern Church. The Eastern Orthodox Church embraces a variety of "national" churches which share a sufficiently common tradition to assert that they belong to the one true Church of God, founded by Jesus Christ, that is preserved undivided and true to its apostolic origins. Forms of

Christianity outside Orthodoxy are therefore considered a deviation.

The origin of the Orthodox Church is found in the period before the Roman Empire was officially "Christianized." The empire was from very early on divided along linguistic lines into the Latin west and the Greek east. Scholars have suggested that the difference in the character of Latin and Greek is in large measure responsible for the differences between the western Roman Church and the eastern Orthodox Church.[9] Latin is a very precise language suited to law, while Greek is a flexible and suggestive language suited to poetry and imaginative expression. Thus Rome looked to establish definitive statements of doctrine, while the Greek Church was reluctant to talk about God except in the sense that language can be suggestive of divine nature. As the Roman Church became increasingly legalistic, and to many critics preoccupied with defining the Christian life, the Eastern Church remained opposed to legalism and casuistry and, given its mystical bent, grew increasingly distant from Rome so that eventually in 1054 there was a final separation.

The development of the Orthodox Church is, as well, connected to political developments of the fourth and fifth centuries. When the barbarians from northern Europe sacked Rome, it was the western empire that fell, while the eastern provinces remained for the most part unaffected. Thus Constantinople became the "new Rome," and the center of the Byzantine Empire, which was named after the Greek town of Byzantium on whose site Constantinople was built. The Byzantine Empire continued many Roman institutions, most important of which was that of emperor, who possessed authority over both secular and spiritual issues. At the same time, this authority was seen as God-given, as suggested by how the emperor was anointed by the Patriarch of Constantinople, who, despite the increasing authority of the Bishop of Rome, remained the ecclesiastical head of the Church in the Greek world.

Originally, there was one Byzantine Church, to which all groups within the Orthodox Church trace their historical origins. With the spread of the Church and the conversion of such racial groups as Slavs, Russians, Serbs, and Bulgarians, however, there developed many "national" churches, which, while remaining historically, theologically, and liturgically connected to the Byzantine Church, were ecclesiastically independent. After the Fall of Constantinople to the Turks in 1453, this growth of independent churches was in some measure checked, as the Sultanate placed all the churches under the central administration of the Patriarch of Constantinople. But with the breakup of the Turkish empire in the nineteenth century, and the creation of new nation states, there was a reemergence of national churches reflecting their differing cultural origins.

The Orthodox Church today is comprised of a group of self-governing churches. Within each church, all decisions are made by an episcopal council at which the chief prelate or patriarch presides. While the chief prelate might have considerable influence in the synod, he possesses no absolute authority. Traditionally, the Patriarchates of Constantinople, Alexandria, Antioch, and Jerusalem have the first places of honor, with the Patriarch of Constantinople being called the "Ecumenical Patriarch" in that he calls synods involving bishops of all the national churches at which issues of mutual interest are discussed. Today, the Orthodox Church figures largely in eastern Europe, and is especially prominent in Poland, Czechoslovakia, Russia, and Bulgaria.

Despite the complex political forces operating on the Orthodox Church, it did not experience, as did the western Church, anything comparable to the Reformation. Today, all the national churches see themselves as consistent with the earliest teachings of Byzantine times, themselves traceable back to the ancient Fathers. This is not to say, however, that the Orthodox Church has not experienced change. Tradition is a central feature of the Church and is seen to grow out of the Church's collective life as a living experience that is ever enriching itself.

From early on, there were significant differences between the Eastern Church and Rome. One of these centers on the Trinity. While western theologians saw the Spirit as coming from the Father, and, as a gift, through the Son, eastern theologians insisted that the Father was the single source of both the Spirit and the Son. Beyond this, the Eastern Church rejected the doctrines of Purgatory and the Immaculate Conception, and were especially critical of papal infallibility. But theology was never for the Eastern Church a matter of primary importance, as prayer and devotion have remained central in the distinctively mystical orientation of the Orthodox Church. The Greek liturgy in particular encourages the so-called "silent moment" in which the divine is immediately experienced in a way not unlike what we have seen in various Asian traditions.

POST-REFORMATION CHRISTIANITY

Christianity since the Reformation has been subject to all manner of influences. Among the most important of these is the Renaissance, which awakened within humankind a sense of its own potential, as well as an appreciation for the world in which one lives. Science came to be seen as a way of uncovering the glories of God's creation, and reason was celebrated as the God-given faculty which assists humankind in this enterprise. Thus was heralded that period of European intellectual history called the "Enlightenment," so-named because humankind came to possess new knowledge that laid to rest the prejudices and superstitions of the past. In this context, Christianity became a "reasonable" religion, as ritual, revelation, and theology were minimized to a few simple teachings confirmed by reason. The thrust of this "reasonableness" is exemplified by the Latitudinarian movement in the English Church, which expressed an enlightened tolerance of differing religious views; by the rise of Deism, which asserted that God was creator but denied that He actively participated in the world or possessed divine providence; and by the establishment of the Unitarian Church, which rejected the Trinity and asserted that Christ was merely a man given special divine powers.

The desire to ground Christianity in reason removed, of course, much of the mystery which is a large part of religious experience. It was to bring the "wholly other" into this world and to make it comprehensible in human terms. For some, this was unacceptable. Christianity had from its beginning accepted that God's ways were not to be understood fully by humankind, and that to aspire to such understanding was to run against divine intention. A notable reaction to Enlightenment Christianity, then, took the form of Pietism, which placed great stress on the conversion experience that took place in one's heart rather than in one's head, although its emphasis on the personal God-individual relationship was as much a rejection of theological Christianity as were Latitudinarianism and Deism.

Pietism has long been part of the Christian Church, as there have always been those who relate to God through simple faith and love. As an identifiable movement, however, Pietism begins with Philipp Jakob Spener (1635-1705). Spener himself was a trained theologian, who did not, in fact, reject the established doctrine of the Church, in his case Lutheranism; rather, he insisted that doctrine never take precedence over personal faith. Significant in the Pietistic movement, too, was the development of Methodism, whose originator and chief exponent was John Wesley (1703-1791), and which was largely a response to an English Church suffering through a peculiarly pronounced period of spiritual torpor. Methodism placed emphasis on personal spiritual experience, as members of the new movement were encouraged to share these experiences with the congregation so that its members could spiritually profit. Methodism also stressed social activism, as Wesley and his followers saw their mission to be the bringing of God to the lower classes and as the improving of their lot in this world.

The growth of Pietism, and its emphasis on individual religious experience, must also be seen in the context of a larger cultural and social rejection of Enlightenment values. For many, the French

Revolution (1792-1795) was to be the supreme victory of reason; in reality, however, it degenerated into fanaticism and violence. Reason was to have given humankind the capacity to improve the world for all who live in it, but, as the industrial revolution progressed, and the price of such progress on ordinary people became increasingly clear, reason came to be viewed as the cause of human suffering. The Romantics, while not outright rejecting reason, appreciated its limits, and gave it a secondary role to imagination and intuition. For the Romantics, truth was not to be talked about or logically derived; rather, it was to be immediately grasped. Such a radical shift in looking at the world had an inevitable effect on Christianity. The God of theology was a God talked about, and no amount of talking, the Romantics insisted, could either reveal God or allow one to experience Him. Indirectly, then, the Romantics accepted the notion of a divine presence beyond doctrine and theology, and indeed beyond the defining limits of Christianity itself. Among those Christian thinkers influenced by the Romantics was the Moravian theologian Friedrich Schleiermacher (1768-1834), who, already a Pietist, rejected the notion of religion as "knowledge" for the German concept of *Gefuhl* or "feeling."

A major chapter in the history of Christianity is the North American experience. While concern with the New World in the sixteenth century was largely motivated by the desire for great riches, the actual colonization of North America was directly tied to religion. Elizabeth I might have expressed tolerance towards her subjects on the matter of religion, but there were still limits to this tolerance. Among her subjects were those who insisted that Elizabeth's *via media* was an unsatisfactory compromise that had not taken Reformation far enough. Variously known as Brownists, Separatists, and Congregationalists, these reformers were in time a distinct threat to political harmony and stability. By forcing Elizabeth's hand, as well as that of James I, religious conformity became in time a fact of English life, and, as a result, those wishing the religious freedom denied in England were forced to move to North America in quest of their "new Eden." These Puritans, as they came to be called, comprised the first significant wave of colonists into North America.

The early colonists represented many forms of Protestant Christianity, and thereby established the religious diversity that was to become the dominant feature of Christianity in Canada and the United States. While the so-called "mainline" Churches are present today, there is in any town or city any number of small, independent, congregational churches practicing their own form of Christianity. The striking diversity of North American Christianity comes, as well, from an absolute separation of Church and State, which made religious freedom a fact of North American life. Significantly, though, this separation has contributed to a decline in the popularity of Christianity, as individuals are now left to choose, not just among religions, but whether religion has any part at all to play in their lives.

CHRISTIANITY IN THE MODERN WORLD

Like all the world's religious traditions, Christianity faces particular obstacles in the modern world. In an increasingly secular world, Christianity is seen by many as lacking answers to the very complex problems humankind faces. The twentieth century has been marked by the "death of God," and by largescale defection from the Church. While it is true that charismatic Christianity has become especially prominent in North America and South America, it is still a minority concern, and the mainline churches continue to struggle for new members. Contemporary Christianity is often criticized for how it has become an extension of the larger culture and society, and how it has lost any sense of revolutionary zeal, although at the same time the development of a theology of liberation is a direct response to the social conditions of the Third World, and particularly South America. Prominent on the Christian Church's agenda is the role of women, which remains an unresolved issue, but which demands attention given the radical change in the role of women in society.

Christianity in the twentieth century has not, however, been without significant developments. It has produced any number of important theologians, who have tried to place Christianity in the context of an ever-changing world. Important, for example, is the Protestant theologian, Paul Tillich (1886-1963), who, in arguing that symbols expressing God reflect the culture from which they are derived, has struggled hard to place Christianity in a multireligious context. Along different lines, Reinhold Niebuhr (1892-1971) and H. Richard Niebuhr (1894-1962) place particular emphasis on ethics, and look to see how Christianity can be used to transform society.

Christianity in the twentieth century has also had considerable success in spreading its message into

the developing world, and has married this missionary
spirit with the desire to care for the world's suffering.
Mother Teresa, winner of the Nobel Peace Prize,
serves as a great example to the world, as she works
for the poor and needy in the slums of Calcutta. The
twentieth century has also produced a new Christian
ecumenism, as Protestant, Catholic, and Orthodox are
once more engaged in serious dialogue in an attempt
to find the common ground in Christianity, despite
differences in theology, ecclesiology, and ritual. Central
here are the efforts of Pope John XXIII, who in 1962
called the Second Vatican Council. His message was
that the Church must become more socially
responsible, and he proclaimed that particular
importance must be given to Christian unity. This
remains, however, the elusive goal for Christianity in
the twentieth century.

Notes

[1]Isa. 7:14-17.

[2]Zech. 9:7.

[3]Matt. 3:17.

[4]Mark 1:25.

[5]1 Cor. 11:26.

[6]John 1:1-5.

[7]Quoted in Stephen Reynolds, *The Christian
Religious Tradition* (Encino: Dickenson Publishing,
1977), pp. 662-63.

[8]Rom 8:29-30.

[9]Steven Runciman, "The Greek Church and the Peoples of Eastern Europe," *The Christian World*, ed. Geoffrey Barraclough (New York: Harry N. Abrams, 1981), p. 109.

Selected Readings

Atkinson, James. *Martin Luther: Prophet to the Church Catholic.* Grand Rapids, Michigan: William B. Eerdmans, 1983.

Aubert, Roger (ed.) *Prophets in the Church.* New York: Paulist Press, 1968.

Benko, Stephen. *Pagan Rome and The Early Christians.* Bloomington: Indiana State University Press, 1984.

Benson, George Willard. *The Cross: Its History and Symbolism.* New York: Hacker Art Books, 1976.

Bolshakoff, Sergius and M. Basil Pennington. *In Search of True Wisdom.* Garden City, New York: Doubleday and Company, 1979.

Bossy, John. *Christianity in the West: 1400-1700.* New York: Oxford University Press, 1985.

Brown, Colin. *Philosophy and the Christian Faith.* Don Mills, Ontario: Intervarsity Press, 1968.

Brown, William Adams. *Toward a United Church: Three Decades of Ecumenical Reformed Church.* Michigan: Baker Book House, 1983.

Burrell, Sidney A. *The Role of Religion in Modern European History.* New York: The Macmillan Company, 1964.

Clark, Elizabeth A. *Women in the Early Church.* Delaware: Michael Glazier, 1983.

Evans, Alice F. and Robert A. Evans. *Introduction to Christianity.* Atlanta: John Knox Press, 1980.

Forell, George Wolfgang. *History of Christian Ethics.* Minneapolis: Augsburg Publishing House, 1979.

Gilson, Etienne. *History of Christian Philosophy in the Middle Ages.* New York: Randon House, 1955.

Hellwig, Monika K. *Understanding Catholicism.* New York: Paulist Press, 1981.

Hexter, J.H. *The Judeo-Christian Tradition.* New York: Harper and Row, 1966.

Hillerbrand, Hans J. *The World of the Reformation.* Michigan: Baker Book House, 1969.

Kautsky, Karl. *Foundations of Christianity.* New York: Monthly Review Press, 1972.

Latourette, Kenneth Scott. *Christianity Through the Ages.* New York: Harper and Row, 1965.

Lingle, Walter L. and John W. Kuykendall. *Presbyterians, Their History and Beliefs.* Atlanta: John Knox Press, 1978.

Lynch, Lawrence E. *Christian Philosophy.* Toronto: Canadian Broadcasting Corporation, 1963.

Marty, Martin E. *A Short History of Christianity.* Scarborough: The New American Library of Canada, 1974.

McKenna, Sister Mary Lawrence. *Women in the Church*. New York: P.J. Kennedy and Sons, 1967.

Muir, Edwin. *John Knox: Portrait of a Calvinist*. New York: Kennikat Press, 1929.

Niesel, Wilhelm. *The Theology of Calvin*. Trans. Harold Knight. Michigan: Baker Book House, 1980.

Olin, John C. *Christian Humanism and the Reformation*. New York: Harper and Row, 1965.

Potter, G.R. and M. Greengrass. *John Calvin*. London: Edward Arnold Publications, 1983.

Rosten, Leo (ed.) *Religions of America*. New York: Simon and Schuster, 1975.

Smith, Warren Thomas. *Augustine: His Life and Thought*. Atlanta: John Knox Press, 1980.

Tillich, Paul. *Morality and Beyond*. New York: Harper and Row, 1963.

Todd, John M. *Luther: A Life*. London: Hamish Hamilton, 1982.

CHAPTER VII

ISLAM

VII

ISLAM

INTRODUCTION

Of the world's major religions, Islam is both the youngest and the fastest growing. About 600 million people are today Muslims. Drawn from all cultural and racial groups, the Muslim population stretches from the east coast of Africa to Indonesia and Malaysia. It was intended from its beginnings to have a universal appeal, and certainly it has enjoyed considerable success. Like Judaism and Christianity, Islam is a religion based on revelation: God has revealed His divine will to humankind. The word

"*Islām*" is Arabic meaning "to surrender" or "to submit" and a "*Muslim*" is one who "surrenders" or "submits." Islam is a religion demanding complete obedience to Allah or "the God."

HISTORICAL ORIGINS

The history of Islam begins in 610 CE in the Arabian city of Mecca, when a man named Muhammad began his career as a preacher and religious teacher. Before the time of Muhammad, most Arabs were nomadic, with the largest social unit being the tribe, the members of which traced themselves to a common ancestor. The religion of this period was not unlike what one finds in contemporary popular Chinese religion, a combination of spirit worship and polytheism. Mecca was very much a center for this kind of religious practice long before it was designated the most holy city of Islam. Several generations before Muhammad, the Quraysh, the tribe to which he was eventually to be born, settled in Mecca and took control of it. The chief god of the Quraysh was known as Allah. What eventually distinguished Islam, then, was not Allah itself, but that Islam made Allah the only God.

Muhammad was born in Mecca in 570 CE. Little is known about his early life, although we do know that at the age of twenty-five Muhammad married Khadījah, a wealthy widow about fifteen years his senior, for whom he originally served as a commercial agent. He outlived his wife, and was apparently devastated by her death. Muhammad had several children with Khadījah, although only one daughter survived. Having an unsettled early life,

Muhammad seems to have turned to religion to find comfort. He seems, as well, to have been especially sensitive to the injustices of a tribal society that condoned bloodshed and violence. It is said that Muhammad cultivated the habit of seclusion and meditation in the barren hills surrounding Mecca, and that these solitary vigils climaxed in a series of intense religious experiences. From these experiences, Muhammad received a message which he felt compelled him to preach to the people of his time. Among those things Muhammad criticized, as a result of this religious experience, was the rampant polytheism of Mecca, the injustices of the kinship system, and humankind's preoccupation with worldly things.

Muhammad preached for ten years in Mecca, but had very little success; at best he gathered a few followers around him. This should not be seen as surprising, for Mecca, as a religious center, was forever attracting self-styled religious leaders and prophets. At the same time, it is not as if Muhammad did not make his share of enemies. In attacking the tribe, which was the fundamental unit of Arab society, as well as espousing a universal monotheism, itself a threat to accepted norms, Muhammad was clearly perceived as a threat to the political and social establishment of Mecca. For a time, Muhammad's own tribe, the Quraysh, protected him, but when this protection was withdrawn, Muhammad was left in a vulnerable position and was compelled to go outside Mecca for support. This support he found in the city of Medina, located about two hundred miles north of Mecca. In the year 622, a large group of Medinans formally accepted Muhammad as the prophet of Allah and agreed to fight on behalf of Allah. At about the same time, Muhammad began smuggling his followers out of Mecca, and he himself just managed to escape from Mecca in an event which has come to be called the *hijrah* or "flight." It is from this day, September 24, 622 that the Muslim calendar is determined. Islam accepts that Muhammad received from God permission to fight on behalf of the new religion, and so Muhammad turned his attention to the military conquest of Mecca, which was concluded in 630. After his great triumph, however, Muhammad had little time to enjoy it, for in 632 he died suddenly, leaving the young Islamic community without a leader.

THE ISLAMIC MESSAGE

The message Muhammad preached to the Arabs came to him as a series of revelations, which began during his period of meditation in the hills outside Mecca, and then continued throughout the rest of his life. According to tradition, Muhammad was meditating when an angelic being appeared before him and demanded, "*Iqra'*" or "recite." It is said that Muhammad's response was to refuse, perhaps out of fear. A second time he was told to recite, and a second time he refused. Only when he was threatened by the angel did Muhammad give his consent. What this story makes clear is that Muhammad took no initiative in seeking prophecy, and that he was simply a vehicle for God's message. The necessity of submission to divine will, as well as the notion that Muhammad is the last of God's great prophets, is also clearly affirmed in this story.

What Muhammad received from Allah over a twenty-year period was collected in a text called the

Qur'ān, itself meaning "recitation." Initially, there were four separate collections of Muhammad's revelations, but eventually, under the direction of Zayd ibh-Thābit, Muhammad's secretary, a definitive text was established. The divine origin of the *Qur'ān* is, not only suggested by its title, which affirms the role of Muhammad as a vehicle for God's message, but also in how Muhammad is traditionally viewed as being illiterate and thus unable to make up his own book or copy it from Jewish or Christian scriptures with which the *Qur'ān* shares material.

The *Qur'ān* is felt to be derived from a heavenly archetype called the "Mother of the Book," which suggests how the *Qur'ān* is an expression in time and place of divine will. It is not, however, the first such expression of divine will, and Islam teaches that God has spoken to humankind on a number of previous occasions through his prophets. Adam, the very first man, was chosen a prophet and given a book so that he and his descendents might be guided in the ways of Allah. But Adam, through his own perversity, chose to ignore Allah's instruction and was alienated from Allah. This original act of mercy has been repeated throughout history, as God sends prophets to reestablish the human race on the right path. History is also, however, a process by which humankind repeatedly falls away from the path marked out by divine guidance. The *Qur'ān* is God's final word; there will be no others--simply put, humankind has one final chance. Thus the *Qu'rān* states:

> These are the men to whom Allah has been gracious: the prophets from among the descendents of Adam and of those whom We

carried in the Ark with Noah; the descendents of Abraham, of Israel, and of those whom We have guided and chosen. For when the revelations of the Merciful were recited to them they fell down on their knees in tears and adoration.

But the generations who succeeded them neglected their prayers and succumbed to temptation. These shall assuredly be lost. But those that repent and embrace the Faith and do what is right shall be admitted to Paradise and shall not be wronged. They shall enter the garden of Eden, which the Merciful has promised His servants in reward for their faith. His promise shall be fulfilled.[1]

SHARĪ‘AH

Islam is a religion of Sharī‘ah or "Law." The Law is the effort to make divine guidance as explicit and detailed as possible so that at no time will a Muslim be left not knowing what divine will demands. For Islam, God has decreed a way of life, and this decree is the sole and determinative norm; there is in Islam no such thing as "natural" bases of moral judgment, and most certainly there is no such thing as "relative ethics." In Islam, there is a right and wrong way of doing something, and this is determined by divine will.

It was not long, however, before Muslims discovered that the Qur'ān, which is a relatively short book, did not seem to contain answers to every ethical problem humankind encountered, nor did it make explicit what divine will was for the entire gamut of human behaviour. Thus there developed the religious science of right conduct known as *fiqh* or "jurisprudence." *Fiqh* is the application of general principles to specific cases in such a way that an entire tradition of precedence builds up by which the devout Muslim can govern how to live. Those scholars who study *fiqh* classify all human activity under five categories: actions that are obligatory, actions that are recommended, actions that are permitted, actions that are disapproved but not outright forbidden, and actions that are absolutely forbidden.

The most important of all *fiqh* scholars was Muhammad ibn-Idris al-Shāfi'i (767-820), a brilliant legal authority and polemicist, who was responsible for systematizing *fiqh*. This systematization is known as the "Roots of the Law," which outlines four major sources of *fiqh* arranged in order of precedence.

1. *Qur'ān*

These are the words of Allah, and no other authority may supercede them; as Allah tells Muhammad, "This Book is not to be doubted. It is a guide for the righteous who have faith in the unseen."[2] If, on a given subject, there are clear *Qur'ānic* commandments, these commandments prevail over all else. As already mentioned, though, the scope of such commandments is small, and it was this that led to the science of Islamic jurisprudence.

2. *Sunnah*

The *Qur'ān* is not an easy text to understand. Not surprisingly, therefore, early Muslim scholars turned to Muhammad's life as a model by which the

Qur'ān could be made more comprehensible. This research gave rise to *Sunnah*, which refers to the words and actions of the Prophet. Where it could be established on the basis of reliable reports that the Prophet had acted in a certain way in a certain set of circumstances or judged a certain way when faced with a particular kind of decision, such precedent constituted an obligation upon Muslims to govern their own lives accordingly. The thinking behind *Sunnah* was that Muhammad, as the direct receiver of *Qur'anic* revelation, could not possibly behave in any way contradictory to divine will, and therefore what he did and said constituted an elaboration on the *Qur'an* itself.

By the time of al-Shāfi'i, there were many oral reports of *Sunnah* circulating in the Islamic community, and there was widespread disagreement as to what was authoritative. Not uncommon was the view that, while there is no definite indication that the Prophet had done something, one can assume that, if the Prophet had been in such a situation, he would most certainly have acted in a certain way. To counter such fabricated *Sunnah*, there developed the idea of *hadīth*. A *hadīth* is an oral report of something the Prophet did or said, and each *hadīth* has two parts, the *matn* or "text," which is the actual account of the Prophet's actions, and the *isnād* or "foundation," which is the chain of authorities by which the text has come down. The science of *hadīth* focuses, therefore, on determining what constitutes *matn* and on the trustworthiness of the process of authentication. Reports that could not be verified as going back unbroken to the prophet were considered suspect. While the science of *hadīth* remains central to Islam to this day, Sunni Muslims recognize as particularly important the so-called "Six Books" of hadīth which were assembled during the ninth century.

3. *Qiyās* or Analogical Reasoning

The *Qur'ān* and *Sunnah* are fixed and unchanging; the world is not. *Qiyās* is therefore the application to a new problem of a principle underlying a decision found in the *Qur'ān* or the *Sunnah*. *Qiyās* allows, in other words, the extension of implications of an explicit rule of law. Two obvious examples in this regard are the *Qur'ānic* prohibitions against gambling and wine, which are extended to prohibitions against all games of chance and all alcoholic beverages.

4. *Ijmā'* or Consensus of Community

Ijmā' is in large measure related to *qiyās*. There is the recognition in Islam that there are a lot of loose ends in determining what exactly divine will intends. Thus it became common practice by the tenth century for the *imāms* or holy men to address problems together, and, based on precedent, to come to a common conclusion. As well as the principles of *qiyās*, then, decisions of the *imāms* came to be built in to the tradition, and thus what past *imāms* had decided became precedent for present decisions.

ISLAMIC PIETY

Religious obligations, as they express submission to divine will, are, in the Muslim world, of two sorts: moral or ethical and ceremonial. The moral or ethical obligations are, as we have seen, articulated through *Sharī'ah*. Ceremonial obligations, which entail specific acts of piety, are referred to as the "Five Pillars of Faith," and constitute the most visible marks of Islam. Each of these obligations stresses the nature of God's relationship with each individual believer. The "Pillars of Faith" are, however, far more than mechanical ritual, and Islam makes clear that empty adherence to ritual is the worst form of hypocrisy. Each act demands the free and willing commitment of the participant.

1. Profession of Faith *(Shahādah)*

Declaration of faith is the first obligation of the Muslim. It is obligatory for every Muslim to give a public testimony of faith in the unity of God and the prophethood of Muhammad. The customary formula reads, "I testify that there is no God but the one God, and Muhammad is His prophet." Every Muslim must repeat this formula once with true conviction as a visible sign of being a part of the Islamic community, although in reality Muslims repeat this formula many times a day. The conviction that God is unity or oneness suggests the perfection of God, which surpasses anything that humankind can conceive. Consistent with this, *mosques*, which are Muslim places of worship, contain no pictures or icons depicting God; for a Muslim such a thing is unthinkable and blasphemes the perfection of God.

2. Ritual Prayer *(Salāh)*

Muhammad placed greater significance on prayer than on any other religious duty. In Islam there is private prayer, which is subject to no regulation, and *Salāh* or public ritual prayer. *Salāh* demands that every adult Muslim of sound mind and body pray five times a day (daybreak, noon, mid-afternoon, after sunset, before retiring). At appointed times of prayer, the *mu'adhdhin* summons the surrounding community to devotion. While there are slight differences for each time of the day, the prayer always proceeds the same way. The worshipper begins in a standing position facing Mecca with his hands crossed before him. As the prayer proceeds, he assumes positions of kneeling and then of bowing in full prostration with forehead touching the earth. As well as an intimate conversation with God, *Salāh* is a further visible sign of submission to God's will. As such, it is performed only when one is in a state of purity, and therefore the prayer is always preceded with ritual cleansing with water or sand. On Fridays, the Muslim holy day, there is special value given to the performance of *Salāh* that takes place in community with others at the *mosque*. Here the word "*mosque*" has particular significance, as it means "place of prostration." At the *mosque*, the *imāms* have the additional responsibility of leading the congregation in prayer.

3. Fasting during the Month of Ramadān (*Şawm*)

Ramadān is the ninth month of the Islamic calendar, and is considered especially holy, for it marks that period when Muhammad received his first revelations from God. During this month, a Muslim is expected to fast from first light until the sun is set; this means that one refrain from eating, drinking, smoking, and even swallowing one's own saliva. It also demands that one refrain from sexual activity. The purpose of fasting is to gain control over one's carnal appetites, which so often lead one astray. *Şawm* is particularly difficult when it falls during the hot season, although Islam allows exceptions for the sick or those who must perform strenuous physical exercise. These persons are expected to make up for missing *Ramadān* when they are physically capable.

4. Almsgiving *(Zakāt)*

Charity is a further expression of submitting to God's will. To give to those who are needy is partially to give back to God what He has given to humankind. Islam understands that what the individual possesses is fundamentally God's and really only on loan. *Zakāt* is therefore to use God's gifts properly. *Zakāt* is not a voluntary thing, and in traditional Islamic states is collected as a religious tax.

5. Pilgrimage to Mecca *(Ḥajj)*

The last of the "Five Pillars of Islam" is *Ḥajj* or pilgrimage to Mecca, the most holy city of Islam; as Muhammad is told, "Exhort all men to make the pilgrimage . . . . they will come to avail themselves of many a benefit and to pronounce on the appointed days the name of Allah over the beasts which He has given them."[3] *Ḥajj* demands that each healthy adult Muslim of either sex once in a lifetime make this journey of piety. The *Ḥajj* must take place only on certain days of the twelfth month of the lunar calendar *(Dhū-al-Ḥijjah)*. Each pilgrim must wear a special garb of two pieces of white cloth, symbolizing that in the presence of God all persons are equal. Central to the *Ḥajj* is the circumambulation of the *Kaʻbah*, which, for Muslims, is considered the center of the world. The *Kaʻbah* or "cube" is the "House of God," originally believed to have been built by Adam, swept away by the flood, and then rebuilt by Abraham and Ishmael. Also important is the

touching of a black stone located at one corner of the
Ka'bah. This stone is believed to have been given to
Abraham by Gabriel. Originally white, it has been
turned black by humankind's sins.

THE GOD-INDIVIDUAL RELATIONSHIP

The relationship between Allah and each
Muslim is a simple one, as the basic themes of Islam
center on God's great mercy towards humankind,
humankind's continued ingratitude to God, God's great
creative powers, as evidenced in the world, the
resurrection of the dead at the end times, the terrors
of Hell and the eternal joy of Paradise, and, most
important, humankind's absolute submission to God.
An overriding issue for Islam here is the role of
humankind in relation to the omnipotent power of
God. The ultimacy of God is explicit in the *Qur'ān*:

All that is in heaven and earth gives glory
to Allah He is the Mighty, the Wise One.
His is the kingdom of the heavens and the
earth. He ordains life and death and has
power over all things.
He is the first and the last, the visible and
the unseen. He has knowledge of all things.[4]

Despite this ultimacy, however, each individual
remains responsible for his or her own spiritual
destiny. This responsibility Islam makes central in
returning repeatedly to the rewards and punishments
meted out on the final Day of Judgment:

When the sky is rent asunder; when the
stars scatter and the oceans roll together;
when the graves are hurled about; each soul
shall know what it has done and what it has
failed to do.

O man! What evil has enticed you from
your gracious Lord, who created and
proportioned you, and moulded your body to
His will?

Yes, you deny the Last Judgment. Yet
there are guardians watching over you, noble
recorders who know of all your actions.

The righteous shall surely dwell in bliss.
But the wicked shall burn in Hell-fire upon
the Judgment-day: they shall not escape.

Would that you knew what the Day of
Judgment is! Oh, would that you knew what
the Day of Judgment is! It is the day when
every soul will stand alone and Allah will
reign supreme.[5]

The notion of reward and punishment points, of
course, to the central theological problem of reconciling
divine omnipotence with human freewill, which is
especially focused in Islam, given its emphasis on the
transcendence of God and the demand for human
submission to divine will. Why, in other words, does
an absolute God allow evil? In allowing evil, does God
not predestinate certain individuals to salvation and
others to damnation? This is a problem which Islamic
theologians grapple with in a way not unlike their
Christian counterparts; in the end, though, they are
left having recourse to the hidden purpose of God.
Important is what goes on in the heart of the
believer. This truth, which the believer accepts and

by which believers govern their lives, will in its working always remain a mystery, given the immeasurable distance between God and humankind.

One thing does remain prominent in Islam. The stress on judgment in Islam may leave the impression that God is a demanding and unfeeling taskmaster, quick to anger and slow to forgive. Nothing could be further from the truth, for Allah is always identified as "the Compassionate, the Merciful." God will always forgive, but forgiveness carries a condition. At the Day of Final Judgment when all are resurrected, "Allah's promise shall be fulfilled. He gives being to all His creatures, and in the end He will bring them back to life, so that He may justly reward those who have believed in Him and done good works."[6]

DEVELOPMENT OF ISLAM

With the death of Muhammad, the young Islamic community experienced a period of crisis. Certainly Muslims were not prepared for his death, and it was therefore necessary to find quickly another leader to continue Muhammad's work. Thus the Islamic community chose a *caliph* or "successor." The first four *caliphs* were all early converts to Islam, and the history of this period of Islam is a complicated one. There was first a consolidation of Islamic power and then a subsequent expansion of Islam, which was really a concomitant of Arab expansionism of the seventh century. While schism was found early on in Islam, it was not a significant factor until the fourth *caliphate* of 'Ali, the son-in-law and cousin of the Prophet. With the death of 'Ali, it was asserted by his followers that 'Ali represented a line of direct descent from Muhammad, and that the *caliph* could therefore only be one of 'Ali's descendents and therefore one of Muhammad's. In this regard, there developed the notion that this *imām* was more than a simple *caliph*, whose authority was derived from the Islamic community. There was now an acceptance, on the part of some Muslims, that there was a line of *imāms* originating with Muhammad, which had the same power and authority as Muhammad to determine doctrine and belief; revelation had not, in other words, ceased with Muhammad.

Such a claim split the Muslim community. Those who accepted the new beliefs came to be known as *Shī'ah* ("party"), while those who remained true to the original teachings were known as *Sunnis*, or the people of "established custom." In time, as well, *Shī'ah* and *Sunni* have come to differ significantly in matters of theology and law. Particularly important here is the notion of a *Mahdi* or "guided one," who the *Shī'ah* believe will appear at the end times to lead a *jihād* or "holy war" against the infidels. While *Sunnis* have a sympathetic attitude towards *Shi'āh* because they recognize the "divine light" of Muhammad, the reverse is not true, and *Shi'āh* do not consider *Sunnis* true Muslims. Today about 85% of all Muslims are *Sunnis*.

The growth of Islam across North Africa into southern Spain and also to the east into India and what is now modern-day Pakistan comes as the result of a number of powerful Arab dynasties that produced great warriors and a great culture. First among these is the Umayyad Caliphate (661-750), which in the west crossed the Pyrenees into France and in the east penetrated central India. The Umayyad Dynasty was essentially one of expansionism in contrast to the 'Abbāsid Caliphate, which looked to consolidate a multiracial and multicultural empire under one religion. It was during the 'Abbāsid Caliphate that Islamic theology and legal theory flourished, and the center of power was moved to Baghdad. Although Baghdad was eventually sacked by the Mongols in 1258, Islam was by no means dead, and enjoyed a revitalization in the fourteenth century in India. This Moghul Empire has left an indelible mark on India, and in many respects Islam reached its zenith in India during the reign of Akbar in the sixteenth century. At about the same time in Turkey, there began the rise to power of the Ottoman Turks, who retained power over much of north Africa and the Middle East. Eventually, however, the Ottoman empire declined in the face of European expansionism in the seventeenth and eighteenth centuries.

SŪFISM

The Islamic empire of the 'Abbāsid Caliphate was one of wealth and power, cultivated and cultured and immensely prosperous. There were those, however, for whom this worldly success was unacceptable; they viewed it as a corruption of the simple piety of Muhammad and his early followers. Dissatisfied with what Islam had become, a number of Muslims withdrew from society to spend their days in prayer, fasting, and meditation on the Qu'rān. These ascetics looked to devote themselves completely to God, as they saw life as transitory and of no ultimate consequence. Such criticism signalled a desire for the reform of a tradition that in a relatively short period of time had, at least for some, fallen away from its true teaching. Clearly this is the message of Āsim al-Antākī (757-850), who wrote:

> Now I will tell a tale of long ago,
> How first the Faith began, and how it grew
> To full perfection; yea, and I will tell
> How next it withered, till it hath become
> E'en as a faded garment.
>
> . . . .
>
> By Grace Divine I indicate the truth,
> Being taught by God Himself, for that I live
> Within an age become exceeding strange,
> Cruel, and terrible, wherein we need
> Most urgently a statement of our faith . . . .[7]

The essentially negative response of the early Muslim ascetics to this "age become exceeding strange" was nonetheless out of character with Islam, which saw the world as God's creation in which humankind found both fulfilment and pleasure. There evolved, therefore, a response more inner than outer that entailed, not the rejection of the world, but the cleansing of one's inner soul. This mystical tradition is Ṣūfism, so named because the early ascetics took to wearing, as did Christian monks, robes of coarse wool called *ṣūf*. As early as the tenth century, Ṣūfis gathered together into monastic communities, to which both men and women were admitted. This should not, however, be construed as a rejection of the world. The Ṣūfis continued living in the world, but, having experienced the unimpeded love of God, they lived with a radically transformed perception of the world.

Like other mystical paths, Ṣūfism represents the desire to experience immediately the transcendent bliss of God. This is not to say, though, that the

individual merges with or becomes God. Rather the
individual is seen as a mirror in which the light of
God shines. The human mirror is so tarnished that
the divine reflection is hindered; thus the path of
Ṣūfism is to remove the tarnish from the human
mirror so that nothing will impede the divine
reflection. What this entails is the removal of human
ego centeredness so that the individual will is merged
with divine will.[8] This congruence of wills demands
that the individual love God as God loves the
individual. Through such love, one is taken up in the
immediate experience of God which is beyond words;
or, as the twelfth-century Persian poet, Ahmad
al-Ghazālī, writes:

> Love soars beyond the Reach of Human Mind,
> By Parting and Reunion unconfined:
> Whene'er a thing o'er Fancy rides supreme,
> Image is vain, and Comprehension blind.[9]

While early Ṣūfism insisted on the absolute
transcendence of God, consistent with basic Islamic
teaching, later Ṣūfis moved more and more in the
direction of a monism in which all reality is seen as
divine. A seminal figure in this regard is the
thirteenth century mystic and philosopher, Muḥyi
al-Dīn ibn-Arabī (1165-1240), who speaks of creation
as a mirror in which the divine contemplates its own
beauty, and of how each particular of creation is an
aspect of the divine. The end of Ṣūfism is to
apprehend this divine unity underpinning the
particulars of creation. The later fifteenth-century
Persian poet, Jāmī, expresses with particular clarity
this rather radical Islamic monism:

From all eternity the Belover unveiled His beauty in solitude of the Unseen;

He held up the mirror to His own face, He displayed His loveliness to Himself.

He was both the spectator and the spectacle; no eye but His has surveyed the universe.

All was One, there was no duality, no pretence of "mine" or "thine."

The vast orb of Heaven, with its myriad incomings and outgoings, was concealed in a single point.

The Creation lay cradled in the sleep of non-existence, like a child ere it has breathed.

The eye of the Beloved, seeing what was not regarded nonexistence as existent.

Though He beheld His attributes and qualities as a perfect while in His own essence,

Yet he desired that they should be displayed to Him in another mirror,

And that each of His eternal attributes should become manifest accordingly in a diverse form.

Therefore He created the verdant fields of Time and Space and the life-giving garden of the world,

That each bough and fruit might show for His various perfections.

The cypress gave a hint of His comely stature, the rose gave tidings of His beauteous countenance.

Wherever Beauty peeped out, Love appeared beside it;

> Wherever Beauty shone in a rosy cheek,
> Love lit his torch from that flame.
> Wherever Beauty dwelt in dark tresses,
> Love came and found a heart entangled in
> their coils.
> Beauty and Love are as body and soul;
> Beauty is the mine and Love the precious
> stone.
> They have always been together from the
> first: never have they travelled but in each
> other's company.[10]

A number of things are obvious in Jāmī's poetry. First, the world, in being divine, is a place of beauty and goodness; that humankind fails to see this beauty is not the fault of God but of each individual who suffers from self-delusion. Second, through the world one can come to know the glory of God; it is hardly surprising, therefore, that Ṣūfism generated much of the remarkable art of Islam. Third, love remains the essence of creation; this demands that one live selflessly, for, in so doing, one can participate in what is fundamentally divine. Love is, as Jāmī writes, the "unveiler of the Truth, the hidden way into the Sanctuary of God," and the "true Lover" is "pure of heart and holy of life . . . generosity and gentleness distinguish him; carnal desire stirs him not."[11]

It goes without saying that Ṣūfism met with opposition from those who asserted the absolute transcendence of God and the absolute authority of Law. For example, the tenth-century Persian mystic, Manṣūr al-Ḥallāj, was executed because he made the claim, "I am the Truth." Ṣūfism does not, however, reject the demands of Law, which one must fulfil as a matter of course in following the Ṣūfī path. The great Ṣūfī commentator Abu Hamid al-Ghazālī (d. 1111), for example, clearly asserts that neither Law nor theology conflict with the Ṣūfī path.

The most visible expression of Ṣūfism today is the *dervishes* ("beggars"), who in their ecstatic dancing lose themselves in the love of God. It is also true, though, that Ṣūfism has in modern times gone through a period of decay, and that many Muslims now see it having little immediate relevance to the problems Islam faces in the twentieth century. Be that as it may, Ṣūfism has contributed an immense richness to Islam that has effectively countered what may have degenerated into a sterile legalism. While few Muslims are Ṣūfīs, few Muslims have not in some way been touched by Ṣūfism.

ISLAM IN THE MODERN WORLD

Islam has continued to thrive in the modern world, and has especially flourished in the Third World countries of North Africa. Reasons for this are many, but among the most obvious is that Islam teaches an equalitarianism especially attractive to those who have little when compared to those who have much. Islam has struggled to adapt itself to the modern world, and in a country like Turkey there has been a complete split between religion and state. In other countries, such as Saudi Arabia, there has been an attempt to retain as much of traditional teaching as possible, while recognizing at the same time that the modern world cannot be ignored and that the modern world has much to offer. In very recent times, however, and especially amongst the *Shī'ah* minority,

there has been an increasing call to return to the
purity of *Qur'ānic* teaching, and this has in turn led
to a zeal that for many westerners is especially
frightening. The present conditions in Iran are
perhaps the most visible expression of this extremism.
Underpinning such conditions is the desire to return
to the simplicity that has characterized Islam from its
beginnings, but which is seen, in the modern world, to
be repeatedly compromised.

Notes

[1] *The Koran*, translated N.J. Dawood (1956; rpt.
Harmondsworth: Penquin, 1977), p. 35 (19:53).

[2] Ibid., p. 334 (2:1).

[3] Ibid, p. 403 (22:23).

[4] Ibid., p. 107 (57:1).

[5] Ibid., p. 16 (82:1).

[6] Ibid., p. 64 (10:1).

[7] Quoted in A.J. Arberry, *Ṣūfism: An Account of
the Mystics of Islam* (1950; rpt. London: Unwin
Paperbacks, 1979), p. 31.

[8] From Neils C. Nielsen Jr. et al, *Religions of
the World* (New York: St. Martin's Press, 1983), pp.
640-641.

[9] Quoted in Arberry, p. 103.

[10] *Mysticism: A Study and An Anthology*, ed.
F.C. Happold (1963; rpt. Harmondsworth: Penguin,
1981), pp. 252-253.

[11]Ibid., pp. 253-254.

Selected Readings

Ali, Maulana Muhammad. *A Manual of Hadith.* London: Curzon Press, Ltd. 1978.

Andrae, Tor. *Mohammed: The Man and His Faith.* Trans. Theophil Menzel. New York: Harper and Row Publishers, 1960.

Arberry, A.J. *Sufism: An Account of the Mystics of Islam.* Boston: George Allen and Unwin, 1979.

Beck, Lois and Nikki Keddie (eds.) *Women in the Muslim World.* Cambridge: Harvard University Press, 1978.

Chittick, William C. *The Sufi Path of Love: The Spiritual Teachings of Rumi.* Albany: State University of New York Press, 1983.

Cragg, Kenneth and R. Marston Speight. *Islam from Within: Anthology of a Religion.* Belmont, California: Wadsworth Publishing Company, 1980.

Dawood, N.J. (trans.) *The Koran.* New York: Penguin Books, 1980.

Esposito, John L. *Women in Muslim Family Law.* Syracuse: Syracuse University Press, 1982.

Fry, C. George and James R. King. *Islam: A Survey of the Muslim Faith.* Michigan: Baker Book House, 1980.

Gibb, H.A.R. *Mohammedanism.* 2nd Edition, 1966; rpt. London: Oxford University Press, 1979.

Goldziher, Ignaz. *Introduction to Islamic Theology and Law.* Trans. Andras and Ruth Hamori. New Jersey: Princeton University Press, 1981.

Haddad, Yvonne Yazbeck. *Contemporary Islam and The Challenge of History.* Albany: State University of New York Press, 1982.

Hourani, George F. (ed.) *Essays on Islamic Philosophy and Science.* Albany: State University of New York Press, 1975.

Lazarus-Yafeh, Hava. *Some Religious Aspects of Islam.* Leiden, The Netherlands: E.J. Brill, 1981.

Lings, Martin. *Muhammad: His Life Based on the Earliest Sources.* New York: Inner Traditions International Ltd., 1983.

MacEoin, Denis and Ahmed Al-Shahi (eds.) *Islam in the Modern World.* Kent: Croom Helm Ltd., 1983.

McDonough, Sheila. *Muslim Ethics and Modernity.* Waterloo: Wilfred Laurier University Press, 1984.

Minai, Naila (ed.) *Women in Islam: Tradition and Transition in the Middle East.* New York: Seaview Books, 1981.

Morewedge, Parviz (ed.) *Islamic Philosophical Theology.* Albany: State University of New York Press, 1979.

Pipes, Daniel. *In the Path of God: Islam and Political Power.* New York: Basic Books, Inc., 1983.

Rahman, Fazlur. *Islam and Modernity.* Chicago: The University of Chicago Press, 1982.

Rahman, Fazlur. *Major Themes of the Qur'an.* Minneapolis: Bibliotheca Islamica, 1980.

Roberts, D.S. *Islam: A Concise Introduction.* San Francisco: Harper and Row, 1981.

Sachedina, Abdulaziz Abdulhussein. *Islamic Messianism.* Albany: State University of New York Press, 1981.

Schacht, Joseph. *An Introduction to Islamic Law.* Oxford: Oxford University Press, 1979.

Swartz, Medin L. (ed.) *Studies on Islam.* New York: Oxford University Press, 1981.

Watt, W. Montgomery. *Muhammad: Prophet and Statesman,* 1961; rpt. London: Oxford University Press, 1964.

CHAPTER VIII

CONCLUSION

VIII

SOME CONCLUDING REMARKS

At the beginning of this text, the question was raised, "what is religion?" After looking at a number of the world's religions, perhaps the best answer is to say there is no such thing as religion but only religions, and that the desire to reduce the vast diversity of what humankind calls religious experience to a few salient features is to take away the richness that makes the world's religions subjects worthy of study.

It has often been argued that, while an introductory course in geography introduces geography and an introductory course in anthropology introduces anthropology, an introductory course in Religious

Studies introduces not religion but religions. This is a position with much merit, for it stands opposed to the all too easy tendency to see all religions as fundamentally the same or at least all other religions as the same as one's own. The stress on religions affirms difference, and few scholars would argue with the notion that differences are much more interesting than similarities.

In this study of religions, one thing is obvious: there are no absolute answers. The various religions of the world aim to connect us to a reality that completely overturns everything defining the conventional world in which we live. Obviously, then, these religions, which are couched in the constructs of conventional understanding, will reach a point beyond which they cannot go. Telling in this regard is one of the simple yet profoundly suggestive stories of the Buddha, which might also serve as an appropriate conclusion to a consideration of the world's religions.

When asked about the nature of the *Dharma*, Śākyamuni tells of the man facing the prospect of having to cross a dangerous river. Not able to swim, he gathers together twigs and branches, in fact, anything on which he can get his hands, and fits them together into a raft. The raft, when it is finished, is lop-sided, leaks, and is terribly inefficient; it does, however, get the man across the river. For Śākyamuni, the *Dharma* is the raft; for our purposes, we could say any religion is the raft. Just as the raft will get one across the river if one has confidence in it, so too will religion.

Religion has a purpose, and as long as one believes it will fulfil that purpose, it will function. If, however, one does not believe in one's religion, the

religion will fail, just as does Śakyamuni's raft. As
well, if one looks too closely at the raft, the holes
become obvious and one will never get on it. And,
finally, once on the other side, the nature of the raft
really does not matter. Once the goal is achieved,
whether it be salvation, mokṣa, or Nirvāṇa, how one
reaches it becomes inconsequential, unless one is Jesus
or the Buddha, who leaves behind a raft that others
can use.

The significance of this story is to caution one
not to look for water-tight compartments in religion -
they simply do not exist. It is worth remembering
that, when one does attempt to define absolutely the
fabric of any religion, one runs up against the
contradiction and paradox that reveal how, in dealing
with the divine, humankind's conventional efforts are
ultimately found wanting.

Despite the difficulties inherent in studying the
world's religions, such study is vitally important
because all religions address the tremendous problems
we face in the modern world. At the same time,
though, the messages of the world's religions that
seemed so safe and comforting fifty years ago are
found wanting today, and seem somehow out of touch
with the realities of the modern world. The problems
which humankind faces seem too large for anyone
either to comprehend or to address in any kind of
meaningful or significant way. Yet the crisis for
religion in its inability to respond to these problems is
by no means new, and the size of our problems today
are really no bigger than those faced by men and
women a thousand years ago. One must remember
that, however we see the world, it is conditioned by
the subjective context in which we place it. With his

limited horizons, the individual living in the Middle
Ages saw the Black Death as something of the same
monumental proportions as we view nuclear holocaust.

The point is that throughout history religion
has not died out, but has remained a constant for
humankind during its hours of greatest crisis. In the
way religion in the past answered humankind's needs
is a way that religion can respond in today's world.
Religion is based on tradition, on the view that, while
there are certain constants, there is always new
interpretation and adaption. Thus the prophet of old
still speaks to us, albeit how the prophet's message
conditions our lives will be different than for people
twenty-five hundred years ago.

One thing, however, is unique to our time by
comparison to former times. Our problems might not
be bigger, but we are certainly much more aware of
them. Modern communication brings the famine of
Ethiopia and the wars of the Middle East directly into
our living rooms. This tends to make things bigger
than they really are, and gives the impression that the
world is worse off now than it ever has been. Thus
the world's religions feel more obliged than ever to
give answers.

Some revert to a basic fundamentalism, insisting
on the absolute validity of tradition in the face of
change; others try to adapt to new circumstances
radically different from those existing during their
"formative" stages. Both responses face considerable
difficulty. Religions that try to hold back the modern
world often become in time reactionary and coercive,
and do not therefore meet the immediate religious
needs of modern people. Those religions that allow for
accommodation may find themselves in a similar

situation, only because they have allowed for the erosion of the values and ideals that gave them identity.

The purpose of this book has been to introduce some of the immense richness that comprises the world's religious traditions, which stand as a remarkable testimony of the human desire to expand inwardly. The message of the world's religions is that the answer to the problems we face is found, not in expanding outwards into the universe, but in looking within to come to grips with who we are and how we relate to the universe in which we live.

It may seen an oversimplification to say that the world's religions aim to bring out the best of humankind. But such would seem to be so, given their concern with wholeness, completeness, security, and fulfilment, ideals that draw humankind together. This, however, begs the question why the world's religions have a history of doing the exact opposite. Religious wars are a norm of history, and religion has repeatedly been used to justify cruelty and inhumanity. One possible explanation here is that religion never stands alone; it is inevitably tied to politics, to social issues, and to personal prejudice. Yet this explanation has a certain facile quality about it. After all, Islam espouses the *jihad* or "holy war" against the infidels, Jehovah has through history been a wrathful God, and both Śiva and Viṣṇu possess dark and destructive sides. There is no final answer to this problem either, except to point out that once more religion leads to contradiction and paradox. Allah may demand the *jihad* but Allah is also merciful; Jehovah might destroy His enemies but He has a concern for all humankind; and, while Śiva and

Viṣṇu destroy, they also create. Once more, then, we are backed into a corner from which our conventional way of looking at things allows no escape.

To be human is to be limited and not to know. Religion is that dimension of human experience through which humankind escapes its limitations and comes to know. How each of the world's religions accomplish this goal is unique to each tradition, and never must we assume that each talks of different things in the same way. All we can assume is that in each one of us there remains the mystery to which we all desire the answer.

APPENDIX

A PROBLEM WITH PEDAGOGY: A COMMENT FOR TEACHERS OF WORLD RELIGIONS

It would be fair to say that the writing of this book has largely come from my own struggle to define exactly what one ought to be doing in teaching a first-year university course in world religions. Like many others involved in this exercise, I found myself often frustrated at having too much to say and not enough time to say it, at having to choose one religion over another, and at being left with a couple of classes to deal with a tradition that at the very least demanded a semester all to itself.

It goes without saying that the task of introducing students to the academic study of religion is a part of the ongoing dialogue to define the scope and methodology of Religious Studies. Indeed the question of purpose in Religious Studies remains yet to be answered in a totally satisfactory way. And this poses particular problems for first-year courses, which, at least at my university, are intended to introduce the discipline--both its subject matter and its methodology. No one would disagree that Religious Studies is unique. There exists an interrelationship between the study of religion and other disciplines in the humanities and social sciences, which does not exist to quite the same degree among those same disciplines. Thus departments of History teach courses in the Early Church and the Reformation, departments of Sociology, Anthropology, and Philosophy regularly offer their courses in religion, and English departments often have as one of their most popular courses The Bible as Literature. The result is that much of the methodological baggage of these disciplines has reverted to Religious Studies, not that this is necessarily a bad thing--it is simply a fact of life.

This, however, begs the question: does Religious Studies itself have a defining approach or methodology, which can be communicated in the crucial first-year course that may, in fact, be the only Religious Studies course a student takes? As one who has just gone through the exercise of steering through the various university councils a proposal for implementation of a major and hence departmental status, I can attest to the difficulty of this task, especially when having to face my colleagues in the social sciences and elsewhere, who think a major in Religious Studies can be tossed together from already existing courses in the university. No one denies that Religious Studies draws from other disciplines, and that it is at once multidisciplinary and interdisciplinary. But, as has often been said by others, such approaches tend to reduce religion to something other than itself. Concentrating on the social, political, and psychological functions of religion ignores the distinctive nature of the sacred which sets religion apart from other "human phenomena." Notwithstanding the significant contributions of James, Jung, and others, the psychologist sees religion as the product of primordial neuroses, the sociologist looks at religion as an expression of societal taboos, and the anthropologist, as well as the literary critic, finds in religion and religious texts productive grist for their "functional" or "structuralist" mills. This is not to deny that their approaches are not useful; rather they are essential if we wish to understand as fully as possible the nature of religion and religious life. But the study of religion is more than just analysis, for religion itself is a matter of conviction, feelings, and action, which belie intellectual analysis and therefore go beyond academic study.

An alternative to the so-called "secular" disciplines is what goes on in Religious Studies. One looks to present each religion as important to the believer and as no more important than any other religion. In this way one avoids the position so easy for the committed believer to adopt--"that my religion possesses the whole truth and all other religions possess only partial truth." At the same time, however, there is something vaguely unsettling about the way such a position suggests an absolute truth that lies behind all visible religious manifestations. This, moreover, flies full in the face of how, for a particular believer, what he believes and how he sees the world is true and vital in a way no other religion can be. Put another way, the believer sees no place in his religion for partial truth: what he believes is fully and absolutely true.

Perhaps a better way of expressing the equality of religions, as well as the objective way in which they should be treated, is to say that the individual believer's religion is true, and that in any discussion of this religion, in a classroom or otherwise, this stands as a given. The basic approach here is to look outward at the world through the eyes of the believer. One accepts, of course, that this is an impossible ideal, in that one can never fully shed the tradition in which one actively participates or which indirectly influences and shapes one's values because it is deepseated in a particular cultural context. More disturbing, though, is the question of whether one can truly treat all religions in this fashion. As more than one commentator has observed, this approach, which reveals the very diversity of religion, also supports the idea that religion is merely subjective and illusory, a product of the changing human mind.

It is perhaps because of this difficulty of defining just what is meant by the objective treatment of religion that the position of the anthropologist or sociologist is so attractive--the scientific neutrality espoused by these disciplines seems to escape the varied truth claims of different religions. Yet there are obvious problems with this so-called neutrality, as have been touched upon. Religion in this context is at best something worthy of study, but certainly not something to live by. The person who insists on the scientifically neutral position, then, is forced into a position of not being able to talk about religion on its own terms, for any religion in doing so asserts its own truth claims.

In the face of this general confusion, one comes to the matter of first-year Religious Studies courses. What kind of course is the best kind of course to give students an appreciation, understanding, and empathy for religious traditions? What kind of course, in other words, allows them to put their own tradition on hold to understand other traditions, or better, what kind of course allows students to use experiences drawn from their own religion to understand the experiences of others from different traditions? Perhaps most important, what kind of course allows students to come away from other traditions, not with the feeling that their own traditions have been threatened, but with the view that their religious lives generally have been enriched; and that, outside of the religious context, they have benefitted in a way we hope for all university courses, and especially those in the humanities-- they are freed of ignorance and have moved outside the limitations imposed by their own culture, society, and religious beliefs? Finally, however, comes the most difficult question. Assuming that all of the above are what an introductory Religious Studies course should do, what kind of a course should it be? Should it stress the neutral position of the sciences, the view that all religions are equal because all only express partial truth, or the ambition to consider all religions as absolutely true, by presenting them as they are perceived and experienced by the committed believer?

It is fair to say that introductory Religious Studies courses tend to fall into two categories. There is the survey course, which is presented to students buffet style, with students getting a little taste of this and a little taste of that--the presupposition is that if they like the pickles they can come back, albeit it means another course. There is also the religious themes course which addresses major categories of religious expression as they are found in particular traditions. I have taught both courses, and I think it fair to say that I have found both to be at once rewarding and frustrating.

We are all certainly familiar with the traditions course. Beginning, usually with the East, one talks about each tradition in turn, speaking as if one is the committed believer in each case--in other words, each religion is presented as true, and nowhere is there a place for value judgments, especially as they might relate to other religious traditions. What one hopes for such a course is best revealed in a commonplace story. Inevitably in any world religions course, one student will voice the question on the minds of every student: what is the religion of the instructor? In this regard, it strikes me the greatest compliment that can be paid to an instructor, given the specific ambitions of the traditions course, goes something like this: "Well Professor _____, after you discussed Hinduism, we all thought you were Hindu; but, after you talked about Buddhism, we thought you were a Buddhist--and you know, it was the same after each tradition you talked about." A simple-minded approach, perhaps so, but in a kind of way it expresses what ought to be the case: that if one expects students to take these religions seriously as something by which people should live, as surely their believers do, then everything an instructor does and says must exude convincingness.

Despite such plaudits, however, one must still ask, is this enough? The basic question, regardless of course, is what is religion? And my experience is that this question is only ever indirectly answered in the traditions course. Usually one races from religion to religion without addressing, except incidentally, the common ground shared by all religions, in spite of their immense diversity. Indeed, it is this diversity which leaves students truly perplexed over the issue of definition. By not addressing the issue of common ground, even to discover there is no common ground, students inevitably see similarities more than differences and fall back on the view so easily held, "that all religions are like my own." It is true that one tends to come back to certain big ideas--the sacred as "wholly other," and the nature of spiritual transformation, for example. But one does so in a haphazard fashion as one lets each tradition speak for itself. I have tried in the past to leave time towards the end of the course for a discussion of the issues that have arisen as we proceeded from religion to religion, or have tried to initiate such discussion as we go along. In both cases, the result has been the same. The overriding concern is to get the material over to the students--to deal with the fundamentals of Buddhism in the few classes available, or the fundamentals of Judaism, or whatever--and this simply overpowers any other concerns. Students get used to sitting there, pen in hand, to write down every word; and when one backs up from the religion itself to get some larger perspective, they are left perplexed. Concomitant with this is that the tradition-by-tradition approach deters student participation. Overwhelmed by the strangeness of eastern religions and concerned that their own religion is not quite as they had thought, students end up in a Zen-like silence, not sure what question to ask. The course deteriorates, in other words, into a spoon-feeding exercise as the instructor shovels information at his or her students.

As a way out of this impasse, I have tried assigning papers that are issue rather than information driven. To make sure students do not simply throw back what is given them in lecture or textbook, these papers are limited to 1,500 words--emphasis is on concise argumentation, not repetition of lecture material. But the exercise has never yet come off. Although students might have some familiarity with the world's major religious traditions, they seem incapable, for example, of drawing even the most obvious conclusions concerning whether or not religious dialogue is possible. And this then leads me to ask myself whether it is fair to ask of students that for which they have no specific participation. One might argue, of course, that the principle behind the traditions course is that it gives the student the background necessary, not for immediate reflection and analysis, but for future work in some future course. But then one comes back to the point that this may be the only Religious Studies course a student takes, and, if anything, he or she should be properly introduced to the discipline. This is especially the case if, as at my university, it is one of those courses designated to satisfy the breath requirement for an undergraduate degree.

The common ground and how it is expressed in various traditions is the focus of the religious themes course. It usually begins with a consideration of what religion is, touching upon in the process such issues as magic and religion, the nature of the holy, and the several "theories" about the origin of religion. Then, in turn, there is a consideration of the ritual dimensions of religion, the nature of religious transformation, what it means to believe, and the relationship between religion and social responsibility. Finally, it concludes by talking about the "other" disciplines--one is introduced, for example, to the psychology of religion, the anthropology of religion, and sociology of religion.

The problem with this course, it seems to me, is that it produces a disjointed view. In its preoccupation with exemplification, it never provides a totally coherent presentation of any single religious tradition. Much of what is used for exemplification cannot be taken from its context without either misrepresenting the concept or the particular tradition from which it is taken, or simply giving an inadequate and incomplete explanation. Instructors are driven to teaching a traditions course whether they want to or not, and end up trying to teach two different courses, and doing an adequate job in neither.

It is worth mentioning, too, that the critical and analytic language of the course tends to be drawn from the so-called cognate disciplines, and the need to explain this language draws attention away from the course's focus, religion If one is not careful, one can end up teaching anthropology or sociology, albeit not as well as the anthropologist or sociologist because one has to do all manner of other things as well.

A final worry for me in this course is that preoccupation with the common ground will stress similarities over differences, and lead once more to the conclusion that all religious traditions are basically the same. Yet to do the opposite--to stress differences--is to force one back into teaching the traditions course-- the differences demand it. Thus one ends up, not only teaching the course one is supposed to be teaching, teaching anthropology and sociology, and a little bit of theology for good measure, but also teaching the traditions course for which the themes course was supposed to be an alternative in the first place. No wonder that students end the course mildly perplexed concerning Religious Studies.

One wonders, then, if the first thing one should admit in a first-year Religious Studies course is that there is no such discipline as Religious Studies, and that, even though there is a thing called Religion, it is a thing to which all manner of disciplines direct their attention. And more than this, should one simply admit, at least to oneself, if not to one's students, that the truly adequate first-year Religious Studies course does not exist.

There is no question that the course I presently teach is an amalgam of the two approaches, with which I still do not feel completely secure. The course is basically tradition by tradition, beginning with the East. This discussion, however, hangs on two other things. First, I repeatedly come back to the basic dichotomy of popular religion--what the ordinary person believes and practices--over against the scholarly tradition, which most ordinary practitioners have little concern with. Emphasis is placed on how popular religion is what the scholar, theologian, or philosopher aspires to explain, while the scholarly level of religion in turn filters down to the popular level to enrich it and to supply it with stability and justification for existence. Second is an emphasis on how religions aim to link us with the divine or the absolutely other, or the sacred, or whatever one wants to call it. And that in this regard, religion is not so much concerned with where we came from or where we are going; rather it is concerned with how we are going to get there. And that, like the Buddha's leaky raft, all religions leak, but they do get us across the river. Finally, I try to make the point that each religion, in linking us to this absolute reality, provides a completeness and therefore a security and happiness that cannot be supplied by conventional, mundane ideals and values.

If I can somehow make these very general issues understandable for each religion touched upon in the course, then I feel I have at least made understandable to my students what religion is about. I may not have given them a complete introduction to the discipline, but, then again, I am not sure that this is possible. My approach remains largely one of letting each religion speak for itself, although, without imposing from without, I try to suggest how each religion does address some fundamental concerns. What the student is left with, I hope, is an appreciation of how there is no one religion more important than another, although I recognize that this is not fully possible, especially for those with strong religious conviction--and that there is no particular way of looking at religion necessarily superior to other ways of looking at religion. In the end, I hope students come away from the course appreciating that religion is far more than they thought, given the limitations of their own tradition. Just to supply my students with this is perhaps all I can expect.

My problem was that, having these ambitions for my course, I could not find a textbook that fitted my needs. So I turned to trying my hand at writing my own text for my own class, and this remains my primary motivation. At the same time, though, I know from talking to others who teach world religions that the issues concerning me are widely shared. I offer this text, then, as another possibility. I most certainly do not consider myself an expert on each of the world's great religions, and invariably errors will creep through and many will disagree with what I say. But this is really part of the exercise of producing a textbook. I would be grateful, therefore, if any teacher of world religions who reads this book and has comment would write to me. I shall do my best to reply to every letter.

INDEX